Praise for *What Was I Made For?*

"*What Was I Made for*, is a powerful devotional that guides readers into a deeper understanding of who God is while helping them break free from cultural lies and distractions. Through daily reflections that combine Scripture, song lyrics, and heartfelt prayer, this devotional book is a gentle call back to the heart of God, urging us to trust Him fully, worship Him freely, and walk with Him faithfully. The author does not shy away from difficult questions. Cultural influences—ranging from performance-based identity to self-sufficiency—are examined in light of biblical truth. Readers are encouraged to lay down false beliefs and embrace the freedom that comes from trusting God's promises. Through this journey, the devotional becomes not just a book to read, but a tool for daily surrender and renewal. Thoughtful and inspiring, this devotional is perfect for anyone seeking a more grounded, intimate walk with God."

Dr. Kimberly Tisi, Professor, Anderson University
Anderson, SC

"Ann Kellett does a masterful job in this book of blending biblical truth, statistics, and studies, all while staying culturally relevant. This is a brilliant work that I believe God will use in a great way."

Mason Leonard, Student Pastor, Mt. Pisgah Baptist Church
Easley, SC

"This devotional offers a deeper understanding of who God is and who we are in Him. It is a powerful reminder that knowing God's character transforms how we see ourselves—beloved, chosen, and redeemed!"

Kerri Jetton, Educator
Easley, SC

What Was I Made For?

What Was I Made For?

Mary Ann Kellett

What Was I Made For?

Copyright © 2025 Ann Kellett

KELLETT GROUP
PRESS

Published by Kellett Group Press
Pelzer, SC

Printed in the United States of America.
First edition 2025.

ISBN 979-8-9997879-0-3 (paperback)
ISBN 979-8-9997879-1-0 (ebook)
Library of Congress Control Number: 2025917093

Created in the United States of America

I dedicate this book, first to God, the one who inspired this writing. Then to my amazing family and friends. Those who have inspired and continue to inspire me through the years. I can't list them all here, but they know who they are. A favorite quote of mine is, "Beautiful Things Don't Ask for Attention." Thank you to ALL my "Beautiful Things."

Also, to you the reader, without your support and purchase this would not have become a reality. Thank You!

"Let this have been written for a future generation, that a people not yet created may know and praise the Lord!"

Psalm 78:6-7

Preface for Bible Study

In the Bible, the book of Psalms has 150 chapters. It is a collection of ancient Hebrew poems, songs, and prayers that come from different eras in Israel's history. The book of Psalms has many different authors, some of which are anonymous. It can be described as a book of poetry.

While there are many different types of poems in the book, they can all be sorted into two larger categories of either lament or praise. Poems of lament express the poet's pain, confusion, and anger surrounding the horrible things happening around them or to them. They draw attention to what's wrong in the world and ask God to do something about it. There are a lot of these lament poems in the book, which shows that this is an appropriate response to the evil and tragedy we see in the world.

The book of Psalms teaches us to neither ignore our pain nor let it determine our lives. God will fulfill His promises from the Bible and send the Messiah. This book is all about lament, praise, faith, and hope of God's people. And like the words of a song, it can soothe our soul.

While lament poems make up much of books one through three, you can see that praise poems are occasionally woven in as well. These are poems of joy and celebration that draw attention to what's good in the world. They retell stories of what God has done in the lives of His people, and they thank Him for it.

In Psalm 139, verses 13-15, David is praying to God, and he says, "I am fearfully and wonderfully made." This speaks of the care and attention with which God has made us. By now, God has made billions of human beings, but we're not mass-produced. We're not churned out in a mechanistic way. Each of us is individually handcrafted, and there is something fearful about how we've been made.

Ever hold a newborn baby and get that sense of awe? The baby is not intimidating and certainly not better at anything than us yet. But there's a sense of awe and fearfulness because you become fully aware of how precious and awesome this bundle is in your arms. God's character goes into the creation of every person.

There's something fearful about us, and this actually doesn't change when we grow up and are no longer baby-ish as we once were. The human body is not just a human body. It is an extraordinary work of art by the God of all creation. However we might be tempted to see ourselves, God actually sees us in a very different way.

In January 2024, Billie Eilish and her brother and producer, Finneas, won Song of the Year at the 2024 Grammys for the *Barbie* album track "What Was I Made For?" Eilish, known for her "dark" alternative music, said in an interview with *People* magazine that when she was called up to do the music she was in a "dark place" before writing the Grammy Award-winning track. She thought her career might have been over. She said also that writing this song helped her through a dark time in her life, when she was dealing with her own identity crisis.

My vision to write this Bible study came from this award and song. Music plays a very integral role in our lives. An estimated 95.6 percent of Americans thirteen or older listen to some form of audio in their daily lives, which amounts to 270 million people listening daily. Music has been proven to do a lot for us. It can reduce stress, ease pain, improve sleep, change our mood, motivate us, increase endurance, and the list could go on and on. But the one thing we have to really watch is the lyrics of songs and how we dissect and relate to them. I lived much of my life listening to Bon Jovi's song, "It's My Life." Oh no, I just told you my age by a song. See what music can do for us?

Much of the most listened to music in this era, depending on which genre of music you listen to, includes Taylor Swift, Olivia Rodrigo, Miley Cyrus, Billie Eilish, SZA, Jon Batiste, Ice Spice, Jelly Roll, Dua Lipa, Morgan Wallen, Luke Combs, Sam Hunt, and many others. There is really no way to tell how many people listen to Christian music over secular, but if you go and pull the stats for some of the ones mentioned here, it's staggering.

On April 19, 2024, Taylor Swift released her fifteenth album, *The Tortured Poet's Department* (TTPD). In just a small amount of time, the album broke all kinds of records. The first week of release, TTPD generated the biggest Billboard debut of Swift's storied career. It sold a stunning 2.6 million copies, including 1.4 million on day one. It made Swift the first artist in the modern era to release seven different albums that have sold at least 1 million copies in a single week, according to Billboard. It has been streamed 891.37 million times. It became the fastest album ever to hit 1 billion streams total.

Unpopular opinion here: she is not my favorite singer and never has been. Now so many of her fan base, "Swifties," will say if you don't like her, you are jealous or that you don't know art or you can't see beauty behind her ability to create thoughts and emotions. Or that you want to stir the pot of social norms. Or that you are a religious extremist. I say this: I think she must be a good business-woman. I mean she began her career at age fourteen, and now in 2024, at the age of thirty-four, she just became a billionaire. You don't achieve that without lots of hard work. Having said that, I will also put this here, not a judgment, because I don't know her and she doesn't know me, but by the lyrics of even her latest released album, I have to think that the billionaire status has not made her "happy." I just don't like the lyrics of her songs, mainly about her world of love triangles, betrayal, and pain. These kinds of lyrics can be depressing to me and almost always cause us to get in "our feelings." And these kinds of lyrics are not good for our mind and soul. I will pick on Taylor a little, just because she obviously has the biggest fan base right now.

In the study you may see a lot of lyrics to different songs, and you will be directed to *a lot* of different Christian songs, written and sung by many different Christian artists. We all have different "tastes" when it comes to the music we listen to. Choose for yourself when the suggestion comes!

The world will always tell us to look at our feelings, look at self, look inward. I pray at the end of this you see God for who He really is and yourself the way God sees you.

The Bible tells us in John 18:36 (ESV): "Jesus answered, 'My kingdom is not of this world. If my kingdom were of this world, my servants would have been fighting, that I might not be delivered over to the Jews. But my kingdom is not from the world.'"

We will also see how as we go through life we gain "labels." Some of these labels are natural, some circumstantial, and some by choice. I believe we all have choices that we make daily, and there are consequences, good or bad, that come from our choices.

When we became "Christians," we became new creations (2 Corinthians 5:17), and I pray that through this study you see "The True You."

The three theme verses for this study will be: Genesis 1:27, Psalm 139:13-14, and Ephesians 2:10. However, you will be going through a lot of the Bible. Let's go!

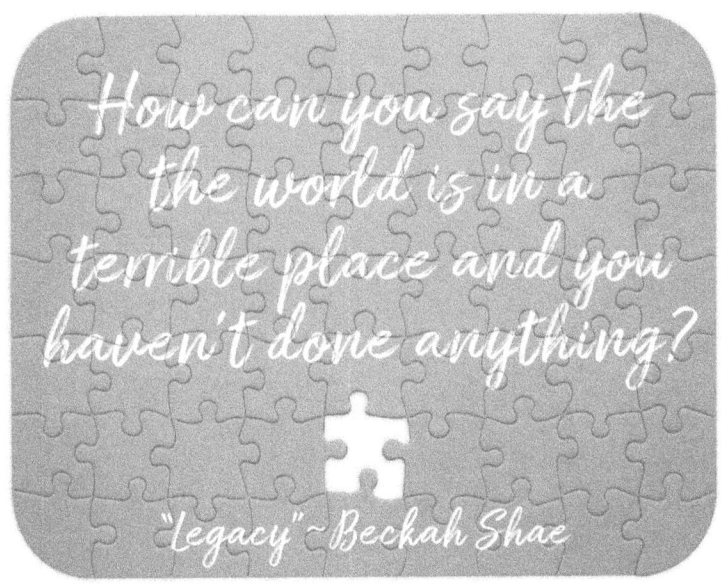

How can you say the the world is in a terrible place and you haven't done anything?

"Legacy" ~ Beckah Shae

I was challenged by the words of this song and grabbed a piece of the puzzle the Lord gave me and stepped out in faith, and started my own business/ministry. I hope this book challenges you to do the same! I reckon our lives to God working a great big puzzle in the sky. He gives us a little glimpse, but ultimately, he holds the final piece to our own puzzle! I can't wait to grab another piece and start working on my puzzle of this season in my life!

Starting Study

Our culture is very interested in the journey of discovering individual identity. Personality tests, dream assessments, even Buzzfeed quizzes are available everywhere you look. It seems like everyone is searching for something to tell them who they are, where they belong, and how they relate to the world. All of us are made in the image of God. We all search for purpose, happiness, belonging, love, meaning in the things we do, whether it's big or small.

Sometimes we search for someone to validate us. We are searching for a better future, something to believe in. I told you in the preface that I would be using a lot of music lyrics and musicians, so here it goes (wink, wink). Musicians usually write lyrics about themselves or others around them! So people (like Rod Stewart) are looking for a reason to believe or (like Poison) are looking for something to believe in. A cause, a role, a sign that we are "doing" what we are supposed to be "doing." We look for directions about which way we "go" next.

The truth is all of us can find ourselves in an identity crisis. How often do we have identity crises? When life changes, as it often does, it may cause us to feel our identity changes with it. The truth is we end up carrying many labels throughout our lives. We may go from a baby to a teen to an adult. We get a job, we become employed, we lose the job, we become unemployed. If we get a job as a nurse, and then we change to a librarian, do we change or does just our title change? Our health could go from "able" to "disable." We can go from wife to mother, son to father. We go from mother and father to "empty nesters." We could go from married to divorced. The truth is life brings us many changes, both natural and those caused by circumstances. BUT GOD (my two favorite words in the Bible).

Many of these changes bring on feelings of fear, feelings of uncertainty, feelings of "I am done" (stick a fork in me), feelings of "Where do I go next?"

But the good news is that when we become believers in Christ, our identity is made certain because God doesn't change. **No longer is our identity based on what we do or who we are but on whose we are. We are forgiven, accepted, redeemed, declared righteous, and so much more based on *who* Jesus is! We now find our identity in Christ!**

We may know this in our heads, but how do we live this new identity out and not revert to our old way of thinking? God's Word speaks so much to this topic.

We should not behave out of our identity; we should behave out of our understanding of our identity in Christ. Never forget who you are in Christ. We can't let "our thoughts," "our feelings," or "our labels" define us. Remember you are feeling bad about yourself or questioning "who you are." Those thoughts and feelings are straight out of the pits of hell and Satan's mouth, and we need to kick him to the curb and remind him "who we really ARE."

In order for us to see our new identity in Christ, we must first see who Jesus is.

The next few days will help us to see through His Word, and His Word alone, not through the world's lens of who we are. Life changes too often to let it label and define us. This is a place in our minds the enemy, who would love nothing more than to steal, kill, and destroy you, wants you to stay "stuck" in, with your thoughts and feelings alone, feeling hopeless, and despaired. Depressed and defeated, looking to yourself or others for validation. Now let's get started and kick the enemy out of our minds, back to where he resides.

Week 1

So God created
human beings
in his own image.

In the image
of God he created
them; male and
female he created them.

Genesis 1:27

Day 1

The Bible says that *all* men and women are created in God's image.
Go to Genesis 1:27 (NLT): "So God created human beings in his own image. In the image of God he created them; male and female he created them."

What does this mean? Exactly what it says: God made both man and woman in His image. Neither one is made more in the image of God than the other. Neither gender is exalted over the other. Our identity was given to us at birth. It is not defined by culture, experiences, or the environment. He is the Lord of our gender and sexuality. There are no exceptions here. The world would have us say we can choose our gender: NOT. It can't happen. That role has already been taken, as noted here. Even God had labels. Here He is labeled Creator.

On this subject my mind goes to a song by Unspoken called "Who You Are." In the song there is a line that says, "You can change who you are." Now if we just took that one line and didn't listen to the rest of the song, where we get the "rest of the story," we could talk ourselves into thinking that it would be okay to change our gender. This song is actually a very empowering anthem about embracing change and finding redemption.

The lyrics speak to the struggles and challenges faced by individuals who are trying to overcome their past mistakes and redefine themselves. (My mind almost always goes to a lyric in a song. Music has always "infected" my mind, which is why I have to choose my listening carefully!)

The subject of gender has become a subject that has divided us, just as the enemy planned. He has a plan for your life too, you know. We have divided because of those groups who have believed Satan's lie of "gender ideology." This lie includes that there is a vast spectrum of genders that are disconnected from one's sex, as born. It maintains that it is possible for a person to be born in the wrong sexed body. These activist groups tell us that we as Christians are being judgmental, and that God is love.

They are only looking at half of the story and tell us that "God is love" and that we should be also. Here you see that one line, not the full story. They are half right. You can go through all kinds of verses in the Bible (1 John 4:8 and 1 John 4:16 are my favorite ones that point to God being love), but we can't just take one line from a song and make the song have meaning. Just as we can't take one verse from the Bible and leave off the others to fit our agenda. That is what is happening among all these activist groups. They are taking one verse and making it fit them, and they think they are okay. This is in no way me being the judge; God has that role. This is a generalized statement on what I see in a divided world, where Christians are being made to look like the judgmental "bad guys."

Now, go and read Romans chapter 2 on God's judgment of sin. This chapter also keeps ourselves in check with our own sin.

If you don't know what the Bible says, you can't defend this before a world that so desperately needs your voice.

Now, if you are reading this and find yourself in this group, let me speak to this right here. The same God that met me in my sin, back in 2010, will meet you right where you are. He will do the same thing He did for me: forgive you! All you have to do is ask, believe, confess your sin, and repent. Repentance means to turn away and move in the ways of the Lord you believe in. If you are a believer, Jesus says this, not me! I don't have that authority!

Now that we have this big elephant out of the room, go into a time of prayer thanking God for how He made you, recalling some of the talents He has given you, the family and friends He has given you. Ask Him to help you have good thoughts, and give time to Him through this study, and give you eyes to see and ears to hear from Him, as these are both gifts from the Lord (Proverbs 20:12).

If this study does nothing more than bring you closer to God, then it accomplished its purpose. I hope that you make the commitment to continue this study and make time for God to show you "who you are."

It's Not About
Who You Are.

↓

It's About

WHOSE

You Are!

Day 2

Welcome back! I hope the Lord showed you *lots* on day one and made you ready to dive into who Jesus says He is. I'm not sure what device or devices the Lord used to bring you to this study. Maybe it was a friend who invited you, maybe it was an identity crisis, a circumstance of life. Just know that on this day, May 3, 2024, I prayed for you!

On day one He gave us our identity. Now for a week or so we will see who He says He is. The Bible tells us a lot about who Jesus is, but we will start with the seven "I Am" statements. Each of the "I Am" statements has significant meaning, both to listeners two thousand years ago and today, as each statement identifies an aspect of Jesus as well as the spiritual needs of mankind. So they tell us who He is and the needs we have.

Read the Gospel of John, starting with John 6:35, where Jesus tells us, "He is the Bread of Life."

Go there now and fill in the blanks.

"I am the bread of life. Whoever _____ will never go hungry, and whoever _____ will never be thirsty."

In this statement, what "two choices" can a person make?

_____

_____

...and...

_____

_____

What does it mean to "come to Jesus" (initially)? If you have not surrendered your life to Him, I pray that today will be the day. None of this study is going to make sense to you if you haven't done so. Romans 10:9 tells us to confess with your mouth, and believe in your heart, you will be saved. He is willing to meet us wherever we are. All we have to do is respond sincerely and accept His free gift of salvation. Recite a prayer, something like this:

> _Dear Lord Jesus, I know that I am a sinner, and I ask for your forgiveness. I believe that you died for my sins, and that you rose from the dead. I turn from my sins and ask You to come into my heart and life. I want to trust and follow you as my Lord and Savior. In your name, Amen._

If you have surrendered to Him today, no matter what you have done in your past, the Bible says you are saved. I encourage you to go speak with a spiritual leader. This may look different for you, depending on who that is. It could be your mom, dad, pastor, friend, whomever is above you spiritually. Go to them and have a conversation with them about what you just did. They will welcome you with open arms and be joyful to help you in the next steps. I am praying for you now as I write this study.

Now, back to the "Bread of Life" statement. Here Jesus is saying what?

That whoever comes to Him, He will be their bread. We eat bread to satisfy hunger and to sustain our physical life. We can only satisfy our spiritual life with a right relationship with Jesus Christ. This is why He refers to Himself as bread. Just as bread must be eaten to sustain life, Jesus must be invited into our daily lives to satisfy our hungry souls.

In Luke 9:20 (go there now), Jesus asks a very important question: "But who do YOU say I am?"

Having true faith goes beyond believing what others think or feel about Jesus; it's about what *we* believe about Him! When Jesus asked this question to Peter, He was asking him to take a stand for Him.

Please don't rush past this and miss it. It warrants prayerful pause and personal consideration. Do that now. We must not only believe *in* God but also believe *all* His Word says; otherwise, we will not take a stand for Him. Who do you say He is?

Go reflect, and we will come back tomorrow to go a little further into the "Bread of Life."

What is
your answer to this
very important question:

"But who
Do You Say
I Am?"

Luke 9:20

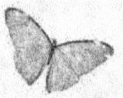

Day 3

Before we get back to the last part of John 6:35, let's not rush this question and dig a little deeper to explore some truths about who Jesus really is.

What does John 1:1 say?

_____

_____

_____

Key points:

_____

_____

_____

Psalm 90:2:

_____

_____

_____

Key points:

_____

_____

_____

Exodus 3:14:

_____

_____

_____

Key points:

_____

_____

_____

Isaiah 44:6:

_____

_____

_____

Key points:

_____

_____

_____

God is who He declares Himself to be, and this incredible God desires to have a personal relationship with you—a reality that should stir our hearts with humility and gratitude. Go listen to the song "Gratitude" by Brandon Lake, and thank Him today.

With gratitude, we can rejoice in God's heartful character described in Lamentations 3:22-23. Write that verse out below.

_____

_____

_____

Back to John 6:35, where God is referencing Himself as "Bread."

What are some "hungers" we may experience in life (i.e., significance, security, status, possessions, etc.)?

_____

_____

_____

Our fallen appetites can lead us astray, leading us to seek worldly satisfaction, artificial fillers. Some of these appetites can and will lead to destruction (drugs, alcohol, affirmation from people (people pleasers), sex, boyfriends). The list could go on and on. Think of one way you may be "filling" your appetite today. If we are not seeking God for our bread, we are seeking worldly food to fill us.

The second portion of John 6:35 brings with it a promise Jesus makes to those who believe:

_____

_____

What do you think it means spiritually to *never be thirsty*?

_____

_____

_____

Jeremiah 2:13 offers a sobering inclination regarding humanity. What does it indicate?

_____

_____

John 7:38 states:

_____

_____

_____

One last time before going into the next day and "I Am" statements. What are the two "active (daily) choices" we can make in relation to this "I Am" statement?

_____

_____

...and...

_____

_____

The first "I Am" statement offers divine declarations: promises Jesus makes to those who "come to" and "believe in" Him. We all have daily choices to make. Make the choice today to not only believe in Jesus but believe what His Word says about Him.

Day 4

Write out John 8:12:

_____

_____

_____

What is the "action" word (choice)?

_____

_____

_____

Let's consider what "following Jesus" entails.

Psalm 81:13:

_____

_____

_____

Psalm 119:33:

_____

_____

_____

Mark 8:34:

_____

_____

_____

James 4:7-8:

_____

_____

_____

In John 8:12, what is the promise made for those who choose to follow Him?

_____

_____

_____

What does Isaiah 59:2 say about spiritual "darkness"?

_____

_____

_____

And Ephesians 4:18?

_____

_____

_____

Wait for it … BUT GOD!

Ezekiel 36:26:

_____

_____

_____

Conclude your time today in prayer and praise. The verses listed below will indeed bring rejoicing!

"Above all else, guard your heart, for everything you do flows from it."

—*Proverbs 4:23 (NIV)*

"You, Lord, are my lamp; the Lord turns my darkness into light."

—*2 Samuel 22:29*

"You Lord, keep my lamp burning; my God
turns my darkness into light."

—*Psalm 18:28*

"He brought them out of darkness, the utter
darkness, and broke away their chains."

—*Psalm 107:14*

"The light shines in the darkness, and the
darkness has not overcome it."

—*John 1:5*

"Blessed are those whose ways are blameless, who
walk according to the law of the Lord."

—*Psalm 119:1*

I hope today has shown you how Jesus is your "light." Whatever "dark" situation you may find yourself in today, knowing this truth about Him should make you want to cut a cartwheel! Well, maybe not literally, depending on your age (wink, wink).

Day 5

Before going onto the other statements, turn to Isaiah 55.

Today, read through it and consider the following:

Note verses that have something to say about "coming" to God, seeking Him:

_____

_____

_____

Note verses that have something to say about "believing" God, seeing Him for who He is:

_____

_____

_____

Note verses that have something to say about "following" God, walking in His ways:

_____

_____

_____

Remember His Word will accomplish that for which He sent it forth.

> "I Am the Bread of Life. Whoever comes to me will never go hungry, and whoever believes in me will never be thirsty."
> —*John 6:35 (NIV)*

> "I Am the Light of the World. Whoever follows me will never walk in darkness, but will have the light of Life."
> —*John 8:12 (NIV)*

Take note of Psalm 46:10: "Be still and know that I am God."

As you consider this passage, what has God impressed upon your heart this week?

_____

_____

_____

Enjoy reflecting on the realities He has brought light in your times with Him. Reflect and thank Him here:

_____

_____

_____

Week 2

Day 1

Welcome back as we continue our study of the "I Am" statements of Jesus. Be expectant for God to show up this week. Watch for ways He is showing up unexpectedly.

This week we will be looking at John 10:9:

"I am the _____: by me if any man enters in, he shall be _____, and shall go in and out, and find pasture."

John 10:11: "I Am the _____. The Good Shepherd _____."

Take time today to read John 10:1-21. Sit and savor God's truths found here. Write out things that are noteworthy: blessings, cautions, whatever the Holy Spirit draws your attention to. Remember to sit quietly in His presence. Where the Spirit of the Lord is, there is freedom.

What are the promises that accompany this "I Am" statement?

_____

_____

_____

God declares His love for you through this "I Am" statement. What is He saying to you?

_____

_____

_____

The thief may be trying to steal something from you today; don't let him. Kick him out. Conclude your time today in a prayer of praise for His unfathomable, undeniable, unending ... LOVE for YOU!

Day 2

Turn again to John 10: 7-10. What does Jesus offer you?

_____

_____

_____

Acts 4:12 states: "Salvation is found in no other names under heaven given to mankind by which we must be saved."

In John 3:16, what made this gift of salvation a reality?

_____

_____

_____

Indeed, God loves us so much. This truth *must* be embraced in faith as *fact* in order to encounter Jesus.

John 10:10 says this: "The thief cometh not, but for to steal, and to kill, and to destroy: I come that they might have life, and that they might have it more abundantly."

Here Jesus stresses that a predator exists. Who is he and how is he described here?

_____

_____

_____

What is this predator's threefold pursuit?

_____

_____

_____

Satan hates God, and since he cannot dethrone God, he targets those who are God's believers. The Greek word for "thief" used in this passage means "one who steals." What do you think this thief desires to steal from believers—to invade, seize, or carry away?

_____

_____

_____

Why?

_____

_____

_____

James 4:7 and 8 instructs believers with a twofold stance when the thief is in pursuit:

_____

_____

_____

What does this look like, to resist?

_____

_____

_____

How can we resist the devil and draw near to God?

_____

_____

_____

What is essential to hold onto? (See Philippians 2:16.)

_____

_____

_____

How can this occur?

_____

_____

_____

Now look at Philippians 4:13. What is this promise?

_____

_____

_____

As we conclude today with a focus on the Shepard and the thief, Ephesians 6:10-18 instructs believers on how to "dress" spiritually as one in God's flock. Envision what this would look like as you put each item on at the Shepherd's instruction. We are protected, victorious as we draw near to Him.

Thank God for His instruction and protection today!

Day 3

*L*et's go back to Ephesians 6:10-18. Read it. This is too much truth to not take a closer look. The whole armor of God. What does that look like for you?

_____

_____

_____

In the Christian life we battle against "rulers and authorities" (the powerful evil forces of fallen angels headed by the devil, who is a vicious fighter). To withstand their attacks, we must depend on God's strength and use every piece of His armor. We need to dress ourselves daily in this armor. Satan checks for weak "undressed" areas.

List our "clothes" (spiritual):

1. _____

2. _____

3. _____

4. _____

5. _____

6. _____

Number one, the devil fights with lies. We must fight him with the truth of God's Word.

Number two, the devil often attacks our hearts—the seat of our emotions, identity, and trust. God's righteousness is our body armor.

Number three, the devil wants us to think that telling others the Good News is a worthless and hopeless task, that the size of the task is too big and the negative responses we might receive are too much for us to handle. But God … the shoes God gives us are the motivation to proclaim the true peace that is available in God—the news a corrupt world needs to hear!

Number four, if we have this piece of armor on when the devil—notice I said "when," not "if"—throws temptations at us, those flaming arrows of doubt, lust, anger, despair, or desire for vengeance, we can hold up shields, and STOP them.

Stand in faith with courage. God assures us VICTORY!

Number five, the devil wants us to doubt God and doubt our salvation. The helmet protects our minds from doubting God's saving work for us.

Number six, the sword is the only offensive weapon in our clothing. All the others are defensive. There are times when we need to take the offensive against the devil. When we are tempted, we need to trust in the Word of God.

Verse 18 says:

_____

_____

_____

How can we pray at all times? One way is to make quick, brief prayers. Make this a habit. You don't have to isolate yourself and say a big long prayer. We just need to make prayer a habit. We have all made it a habit to pick up our phones as soon as we hit the floor. Change your habit instead and give Him thanks for a new day!

Remember, Satan checks for weak spots. Put on ALL your armor today! Just as we can't walk around in nature naked, don't leave home without all your "clothes"!

Pray for your church family, your pastor, and other Christians today! We are ALL fighting the same enemy, but we also all have the same BIG GOD. You can do all things with Him who gives you strength! Go equip yourself!

Day 4

Today we will be back exploring the fifth "I Am" statement of Jesus.

Remember, all these statements are found in the book of John and identify an aspect of Jesus as well as the spiritual needs of mankind. (Trying to keep us reminded of this, it helps us to see our need for Him!)

The fifth "I Am" statement, from John 11:25-26:

"I Am the _____ and the _____. The one who believes in me will live, even though they die; and whoever lives by believing in me _____."

Do you believe this statement?

This statement stands out in the midst of a memorable series of circumstances found in John 11:1-44. Read that now, taking note below of some key points that stand out to you.

_____

_____

_____

Trials of this degree can challenge our faith. They often make no sense and leave us questioning our faith and God. If you were one of the sisters of Lazarus, what might you have felt?

_____

_____

_____

How did Martha respond in verses 27-44?

_____

_____

_____

The powerful reality found in this passage is that Jesus has overcome eternal death. Here is where He declares Himself as the Resurrection and the Life. What was His instruction in verse 44?

_____

_____

_____

There are times when life's difficulties leave us disoriented, depleted, possibly even doubting God; in turn, we may walk around "lifeless." Jesus instructs us to "take off our grave clothes" (put on our armor, day 3, week 2, Ephesians 6-10-18).

We must embrace the fact that the story isn't finished—that He is still working, and will continue to work, in and through each of our circumstances in ways that we may not see or understand on this side of Heaven.

Go to Hebrews 12:1 and 2. What instruction does this provide?

_____

_____

_____

In the midst of life's trials and tribulations, our focus will significantly impact our overall well-being. What does Isaiah 26:3 state?

_____

_____

_____

What is at the heart of this passage?

_____

_____

_____

What is the promise here?

_____

_____

_____

For more perspective, turn to one of my favorite promises in the Bible, Proverbs 3:5-6. What must we do here?

_____

_____

_____

Throughout Scripture we are almost always called to "do something." Here we are called to TRUST. Faith is an action; it actually almost always is a verb! It requires us to _____ and _____.

To "acknowledge Him" in all of our ways is both difficult and essential. He gives us strength to stay the course as we trust and press into Him (Philippians 4:13).

As we close today, consider if there are any hindrances or "grave" clothes you need to take off—things that are lifeless and need to be laid down, entrusted to Him. If today you find yourself "holding onto the past" mistakes, hurts, fears, any clothes that are weighing you down, making you wear bigger-sized clothes than what's needed, take them off NOW!

Have you ever heard the quote "Holding onto anger/resentment is like drinking poison and expecting the other person to die"? They have moved on. Choose today to move on!

If you don't leave your past in the past, it will destroy your future. Live for what today has to offer, not for what yesterday has taken away.

Go listen to the song "I Got Saved" by your favorite singer.

Pray for God to show you what you are "holding" onto, what "grave" clothes you may still be wearing. If you need someone to pray with you about these matters, reach out to someone you trust: a friend or pastor. The One who eternally loves you promises to meet you and give you a fresh measure of life as you encounter Him through His name: "I Am the Resurrection and the Life." May you walk in faith, trusting Him today.

Embrace your future and leave the past behind today. Buckle up; it's about to get real when you embrace these statements and start to believe what Jesus says about not only Himself but YOU!

Let's Go!

Day 5

Let's revisit the fifth "I Am" statement found in John 11:25-26. Jesus posed a question to Martha in verse 26. What was it?

_____

_____

_____

How does our response to this question impact how we walk through life and loss?

_____

_____

_____

Let's read Romans 5:1-5. What truths can be gleaned from this passage?

_____

_____

_____

How can the reality of "suffering" produce perseverance, perseverance result in character, and character result in "hope"?

_____

_____

_____

We can't become "stuck" in our trials or our past. We have to let them build us.

Read Philippians 3:13-14. What is the promise found in this passage?

_____

_____

_____

Keep pressing on today. Pray your way through whatever "circumstances" you may be found in. Conclude today resting in the precious promise of Hebrews 10:23: "Let us hold unswervingly to the hope we profess, for he who is promised is faithful."

Move forward today toward the prize!

C.S. Lewis said one of my favorite quotes: "There are far better things ahead than any we leave behind."

Remember this quote in every season: winter, spring, summer, and the season which shows us how beautiful it can be to let things go, fall.

Listen to "I Believe" by Charity Gayle.

Week 3

Day 1

This week we are going to take a look at the final two "I Am" statements. Let's remember that each of the "I Am" statements introduces us to who Jesus is, as well as to our needs. They also reinforce the reality of God's love for us and His provision for our redemption, reconciliation, and restoration.

According to 1 Peter 1:17-21, what are truths and treasures to embrace as we walk in faith through life? This is a big part of where our identity comes from. Unless you see where Jesus takes us from pit to redemption, redeemed by His blood, made spotless, without blemish. Until we fully grasp this truth, we will struggle with our identity. Believe this truth today!

The sixth "I Am" statement, found in John 14:6, says, "I Am
_____."

In His discussion with the disciples, Jesus's words were both simple and profound. Read John 14:1-14. There are several significant statements Jesus makes to His disciples; what are some of them?

_____

_____

_____

Jesus tenderly speaks truth in order to comfort and strengthen them. He further encourages them in verses 15-21; what stands out to you as encouragement He speaks to those who believe in Him?

_____

_____

_____

How does verse 21 end, and how does this truth impact you?

_____

_____

_____

Jesus desires for us to know Him, love Him, reflect Him, and live with Him eternally. And God has provided a helper for all who embrace Jesus as the Way, the Truth, and the Life as the way to God, the Holy Spirit! Take a run around your room, especially if you haven't done your exercises today (wink, wink)! Although that is enough to run for! What does John 14:25-27 say about the Holy Spirit?

_____

_____

_____

Close out your day in prayer, thanking Him for being the Way, The Truth, and the Life. I hope your spiritual muscles are getting stronger, as we are rounding the corner to the first part of our study on the "I Am" statements and moving on from who He says He is to who He says "WE ARE."

Day 2

Okay, the final "I Am" statement is jam-packed with truth and excitement! Let's look at it now. Read John 15:1-5.

In John 15:1, Jesus declares Himself as:

_____

_____

_____

What does Jesus state in these verses is the result of abiding in Him?

_____

_____

_____

John 15:5 says, "I am _____; you are the branches. If you _____ in me and I in you, you will bear _____; apart from me you can do nothing." Read that again. Apart from me you can do what? YES, NOTHING!

In order to abide in Jesus, what must we do?

_____

_____

_____

Galatians 5:22-23 offer insights on what the "fruit of abiding" looks like. What does it say?

_____

_____

_____

These are manifestations of those who "abide" in Christ. What does it mean to abide in Christ?

_____

_____

_____

In order to bear fruit, we must maintain connection with Jesus: total dependence. While we can "do" things in our own strength, even Christian activities, we cannot bear "spiritual fruit" or experience spiritual growth and maturity apart from an ongoing, personal relationship with Jesus as the vine.

Read John 15:6-17. Who is the One who tends to the branches?

_____

_____

_____

What happens to branches that are NOT bearing fruit?

_____

_____

_____

What happens to branches that ARE bearing fruit?

_____

_____

_____

The word for "pruning" is also translated "cleansing" in other places. What do 1 Corinthians 6:11 and Hebrews 10:22 indicate?

_____

_____

_____

How do we stay connected to the vine?

_____

_____

_____

Go and listen to the song "Be Connected" by Jackie McCullough. Have some fun today, as this upbeat song encourages us to stay connected.

Day 3

*L*et's look at a quick way we can stay attached to the vine.

I did a Bible study at the Cove in Asheville, North Carolina, back in 2023. In this Bible study, the teacher included this acrostic (Patty Stump, "The Names of God"):

A—Adjust

B—Believe

I—Indulge

D—Die to Self (Daily)

E—Endure

This is definitely something to ponder while we are trying to stay attached!

What might the Lord be asking you to adjust today? To believe? Could He be asking you to Indulge more in His Word? Do you believe that you must "die" to yourself daily? Have you practiced that? What does that look like to you? Do you have the mindset that endurance wins the race? That staying where you started doesn't move you to a place of peace? Step out in faith today! Do whatever you have to do to maintain "attachment" to Him!

The next day has passages for each action to help us stay attached. Read those today.

Let's read John 15, verses 5, 6, 7, and 10.

There is a recurring word we see in these passages. What is that word? _____

This is a word that could use prayer and consideration.

As you wrap up today, ask God if there is anything hindering your relationship with Him. If so, address it with God, knowing that He reveals our sin—not to condemn us (see Romans 8:1) but to draw us more fully into a "fruitful" relationship with Him! 1 John 1:9 tells us, if we confess our sins, He is faithful and just and will forgive.

Think of yourself running through the airport with a bunch of suitcases, the plane about to leave in one minute, and you haven't checked in. Think of the "heaviness" you feel. A line in the song "Suitcases" by Dara Maclean, says, "You can't run when you're holding suitcases." Go listen to that. Lay down your suitcases, take off those grave clothes, and run with Him!

Day 4

The next two days will be reviewing the "I Am" statements on who God declares Himself to be before moving onto to who He declares us to be!

The seven "I Am" statements of Jesus:

"I Am the Bread of Life." John 6:35—Our daily sustenance.

"I Am the Light of the World." John 8:12—Our source of guidance. (In Matthew 5:14, Jesus gives us our identity as "You are the Light of the World.")

"I Am the Door." John 10:7—Our protector.

"I Am the Good Shepherd." John 10:11—Our sacrificial savior, our GPS, good personal Shepherd—He is that for ALL of us.

"I Am the Resurrection and the Life." John 11:25—Our victory over death. You can run around the room now. You have permission!

"I Am the Way, the Truth, and the Life." John 14:6—Our access to the Father and Eternal Life. Another chance to take off running. (Man, you are working out today!)

"I Am the True Vine." John 15:1—Our source of vitality and strength. (Thank Him for that now.)

There are two additional "I Am" declarations. I will list those here:

John 8:58: "Jesus said to them, 'Most assuredly, I say to you, before Abraham was, I Am.'"

John 18:4-5: "Jesus said to them, 'I Am He.'"

Notice here, as well as throughout the Bible, these statements end with a period.

These statements should help us to understand that it's not about Jesus; IT IS JESUS.

Go back and read all these statements, and ask the Lord to show you today what He would have you see through each one! Note anything that God has brought to light through each statement. Thank Him for being each of these things to you.

Basking in songs like "Way Maker," "Holy Spirit," "Living Hope," "Because He Lives," the list could go on and on. Thank Him now!

It's Not About Jesus, IT IS JESUS!

Day 5

This is an attempt to summarize *some* of the key points of the past three weeks.

Genesis 1:27 says what?

_____

_____

_____

This is where our identity comes from!

Romans 10:9-10 says what?

_____

_____

_____

1 John 1:9 says: "If we _____, He is _____ and just to _____ us our sins and to _____ us from all _____.

If we say that we have not _____, we make Him a liar, and His word is not in us." (Bold declaration of truth.)

God is the judge of sin, which is found throughout Scripture. Also, John 12:48 says what? Yes, the One who rejects Him will be judged. We ALL have the choice to make. What's your choice?

Galatians 5:22-23 says this: "The fruit of the Spirit is _____, _____, _____, _____, _____, _____, _____, _____, and _____. Against such there is no law."

Read Matthew 17:15-20. Keep in mind He is the judge!

John 15 is packed full of truths about who He is and who we are in Him. Recognizing Jesus as the vine and us as the branches, our relationship should have been strengthened through prayer, Bible study, worship, and fellowship with other believers. Consider each of these aspects of "abiding" with Jesus. In order to strengthen your relationship with Him, is there anything He is impressing on your heart to adjust?

_____

_____

_____

To eliminate (for a season or longer)? This is going to look different for all of us. Only you know what season you are in, at this very moment.

_____

_____

_____

Where would He have you concentrate your time, talents, and abilities as you walk through His will during this season of life?

_____

_____

_____

It is essential to "rightly discern" God's heart for humanity as expressed by Jesus. Remember John 10:10 about a thief?

What is his pursuit?

_____

_____

_____

And God's heart as declared in John 10:10?

_____

_____

_____

This occurs as we "abide" in Christ. As we "abide" in Jesus, what do verses 9-13 of John 15 stress are of greatest importance?

_____

_____

_____

To "abide" in Christ involves our will, choices that WE make. This is a significant word that warrants careful, prayerful consideration.

As we wrap up this part of the study, ask God if ANYTHING is hindering your relationship with Him and your "abiding" in

Christ. If so, address it with God, knowing that He reveals our sin—not to condemn us (see Romans 8:1) but to draw us more fully into a fruitful relationship with Him.

Read Psalm 46:10. Prayerfully pause so that you might encounter Jesus as He reveals Himself to you through this study!

I know this has been A LOT of Bible, BUT GOD ... I know this as well; we could wrap this study up here and not go any further, and you would get a lot of truths from His Word, but I pray you will continue this study and, just like He showed you Himself through this study, you will allow Him (as only He can) to show you who "YOU ARE" through His life-changing Word!

> Philippians 1:6 (NKJV): "Being confident of this very thing, that HE who has begun a good work in you will complete it until the day of Jesus Christ."

> Ephesians 2:8-10 (NKJV): "For by grace you have been saved through faith, and that not of yourselves: it is the GIFT of God, not of WORKS, lest anyone should boast. For WE ARE His Workmanship, created in Christ Jesus for good works, which God prepared beforehand that we should WALK in them."

Don't just those two verses alone make you want to run? That, by grace, you are saved? That He will finish the work that He began in you before you were even born? How often do we start something only to quit because it gets too hard? Too rocky of a mountain to climb? Ponder the last time you felt like quitting but continued instead. Are you in a place you need to do that today? I pray you keep moving today!

This completes section 1 of the study.

Look out devil, here we come, running in. We are running to find out "what we were made for!" Let's go! See you in section two. Run, don' t walk, to get there!

Week 4

Day 1

elcome to section two of our study. I hope in section one you took away a better understanding of who God says He is. And I hope you are ready to let Him show you, through His infallible, or "incapable of error" Word, "who you are" and "what you were made for."

Much prayer and study has been put into writing this, and I pray you give God glory and praise all throughout this study for just how intricately you really are made! Make sure to "dress" (Ephesians 6:11, Armor of God) accordingly every day, as you know your enemy who is walking around like a lion seeking whom he may devour (1 Peter 5:8-9).

We will be looking at lots of verses daily, but our two theme verses will be Psalm 139:14 and Ephesians 2:10. Let's go look at those now.

Psalm 139:14 (KJV): "I will _____; for I Am _____ and _____ made: marvellous are _____ works and that _____ knoweth right well."

Now let's look at Ephesians 2:10 (KJV).

"For _____ His _____, created in Christ Jesus _____ good works, which God _____ that we should walk in them."

These two verses tell us very much that God made each of us with His own hands, designed us for "His works" ahead of time.

I hope that, if you've made it this far in the study, you have made a commitment with God and received His free gift of salvation (Romans 5:15-18). The action of Christ dying on the cross for our sins, which brings salvation from death, rescue from God's wrath, and judgment on sin. If this is not settled, please refer back to day 2 in section 1 before you proceed.

Go into a time of prayer here and ask God to open your eyes to see and ears to hear through His Word. Pray Psalm 139:23-24: "Search me, O God, and know my heart: try me, and know my thoughts. And see if there be any wicked way in me, and lead me in the way everlasting." Amen, now "be still and know." Listen.

Day 2

et's take a look at Ephesians 2:4-9. These six verses precede one of our theme verses, 2:10. Without these verses we would not be here today.

Go there now.

"But God [my two favorite words in the Bible], who is _____ in _____ for his _____ wherewith he loved us, even _____ we were _____, hath quickened us _____ with Christ. And hath _____ together, and made us sit _____ together in Heavenly places in _____, that in the ages to come he might shew the exceeding riches of his _____ in his _____ toward us through _____."

What do these verses mean for us? That through faith in Christ we stand—not guilty—before God (Romans 3:21-22). That the penalty of sin and its power over us were miraculously destroyed by Christ on the cross. God doesn't take us out of the world or make us like robots; we still feel like sinning, and we still sin. The difference is, before we became Christians (label), we were dead in sin (label) and were slaves (label) to our sinful nature. But now we are alive with Christ and have His help, through the Holy Spirit, to avoid sin and live with real joy and freedom.

Turn to Galatians 2:20 (NLT). It says this: "My _____ has been crucified with _____, it is no longer _____, but _____ lives in me. So, I live in this earthly body by _____ in the Son of God, who _____ me and gave himself for_____."

You can shout out with praise just at this verse. Do it now. It's okay, wake up the house. You are alive, my dear friend! We were rebels against Him, BUT GOD.

Now go back to Ephesians 2:8-9: "For by _____ are ye saved through _____; and that not of yourselves: It is the gift of God, not of _____, lest any man should boast."

We became Christians through God's unmerited grace, not as the result of any effort, ability, intelligent choice, or act of service on our part. However, out of gratitude for this free gift, our hearts should overflow with a desire to help and serve others with kindness, love, and gentleness, all character traits of Him. While no action or work we do can help us obtain salvation, God intends for our salvation to result in acts of service. We are not saved merely for our own benefit but to serve Christ and build up the church.

Turn to Ephesians 4:12 (NLT): "Their responsibility is to _____ God's people to do his work and _____ up the church, the body of _____."

Before we go any further today, we have learned what? That we have been given a free gift of salvation. Through faith in Jesus Christ, He took on the cross for OUR sins. We did NOTHING to receive this gift. That we will still sin, we are not sinless, but when we meet Jesus, we should sin less. That we were saved by His grace for the purpose of what?

_____

_____

_____

List some thoughts that the Lord impressed upon your heart today.

_____

_____

_____

Give Him praise and gratitude for what He has given YOU! Go listen to the song, "Is He Worthy?" sung by whomever your favorite singer is. Mine is Cece Winans on this song! He is worthy!

Day 3

*N*ow that we have established that we have the free gift of salvation, and that we did NOTHING to earn it, let's move on to more exciting news about who we are. Thank goodness for our free gift; thank Him now!

In order for us to understand "who we truly are," we must first go back to the beginning once again. We have established that we are made in God's image (Genesis 1:27).

We learned that our adversary the devil walks around for what (John 10:10)?

Yes, he wants to destroy us. He would like nothing more than to take us out, and he starts from the minute we are born.

Satan's strategy is to target your free will hub—your mind.

Let's look at Genesis 2:15-17.

"The Lord God _____ the man in the _____ of _____ to tend and watch over it. But the Lord God warned him, '_____ except the tree of _____ of _____ and _____. If you eat its _____, you are sure to _____.'"

Here is where we are given our first choice: to obey or decide for our own what we will do. Why do you think God placed this tree in the garden and forbid Adam to eat it? Remember Eve is not made until verse 21, which we will look at later in the study. Let's first establish what Satan's ultimate goal is, and that is to destroy you.

God gave Adam the free will to make a choice. He gave him responsibility for the garden and told him not to eat from the tree of knowledge of good and evil. Here we see we were given free will and choice from the beginning. Without this freedom, Adam would have been like a prisoner and not had the chance to do what?

_____

_____

_____

Yes, here is where the word obedience came from! Satan wants you to overlook all your freedom and focus on the one restriction. He wants to plant a seed of doubt in your mind of God's faithfulness.

When we are faced with a choice between right and wrong, remember that God has always given us the decision to OBEY Him. We could do another whole study on obedience, but we are trying to establish our identity in this one, so let's move on! I do want to point out right here that there HAS and ALWAYS will be consequences to sin and disobedience.

Before we move on, we must put Eve in the garden. Let's read Genesis 2:1.

"So the Lord God caused the _____ to fall into a deep sleep. While the man _____, the Lord God took out one of the man's _____ and closed up the opening. Then the Lord God made a _____ from the rib, and he brought her to the man."

We are fearfully and wonderfully made (Psalm 139:13-14).

We have established how sin and obedience entered the world today. We will move on to Genesis chapter 3 tomorrow.

Close today asking God what sin of disobedience in your life keeps you from drawing closer to Him. Journal those thoughts here.

_____

_____

_____

I Praise You, for I am

"Fearfully and
Wonderfully Made"
Psalm 139:14

"His Masterpiece"
Ephesians 2:10

Day 4

Okay, now that we have Adam and Eve in the garden, let's take a look at our enemy. He has been plaguing human history since Genesis 3.

We established yesterday that Satan wants to plant seeds of doubt in our mind, that he wants us to question God's faithfulness.

Before going on, let's take a look at a couple of verses that you may have looked over yesterday, which are worthy of taking a closer look at.

Those verses are Genesis 2:18-20. "Then the Lord God said, 'It is not good for man to be alone. I will make a helper who is just right for him.' So the Lord God formed from the ground all the wild animals and all the birds of the sky. He brought them to the man to see what he would call them, and the man chose a name for each one. He gave names to all the livestock, all the birds of the sky, and all the wild animals. But still there was no helper just right for him."

As I sat on my screened porch writing this, my cardinal family (Raine and Gelia are my Mom and Dad cardinal) was coming back and forth to the feeder. They have been in my yard since we first took up residence here, maybe before that, and I was reminded that God even cared when these animals were made from dust, whether or not they had names. Now, we don't know the conversation between Adam and God about giving the animals names. As the Bible only notes, they were given names, but if it wasn't noteworthy, why would it be added to the Bible? Ponder that when we later discuss how God gives us names. Thank you, God, for my new name! Thank you that, since I was saved by your amazing grace, I have a "new name" written down in glory (Revelation 2:17 and John 1:12).

God cares about even the animals having names; how much more do you think He cares about you? That even the birds had names. At least I don't feel as crazy now after reading this that I named my bird family! Okay, so unfortunately when God made the animals and birds, He also made the serpent. Oh no! Yeah, I am right there with you. I know I likely have a yard full of those as well. I have woods behind my house so ... you know where the story goes!

Okay, we have established man, woman, and the animals and birds. Let's move on!

We are going to look at the question today that Satan always asks us. His number one question that he plants in our mind is: "Did God really say?"

Genesis 3:1: "The _____ was the _____ of all the wild animals the Lord God had made. One day he asked the woman, '_____ ?'"

There you have the one question that will forever plague your mind, that Satan uses as his "playground" in our mind. This question makes us think that we can be our own "God" and not face any consequences—otherwise known as pride!

Let's take a look at what are called the "deadly Ds." Five of them.

Doubt: Makes you question God's Word and His goodness.

Discouragement: Makes you look at your problems rather than at God.

Diversion: Makes the wrong things seem attractive so that you will want them more than the right things.

Defeat: Makes you feel like a failure so that you don't even try.

Delay: Makes you put off doing something so that it NEVER gets done.

Satan wants to create the atmosphere for you to linger in temptation just long enough for you to sin.

We all know the story: Eve partook of the fruit of the tree and convinced the man. (Now we don't have ALL the blame, ladies. It didn't take too much convincing Adam to sin with us.) Satan got Eve to doubt God's Word and His goodness, and it worked!

Now onto Genesis 3:5: "God knows that your _____ will be _____. As soon as you eat it, _____, knowing both good and evil."

Even Satan knows we are made in God's image. And here we see Adam and Eve get the knowledge of both good and evil. Sometimes we get the illusion, in our mind, that freedom is doing anything we want to do. We have the freedom to step out in front of a moving car, don't we? Yes, but we use wisdom to know that that will hurt us. We use wisdom in our decisions because freedom of our decisions causes consequences.

Take me to Jimmie Allen and Brad Paisley's song, "Freedom Was A Highway." Is freedom really a highway? Do we know which way to go on the highway, or do we need directions? "Time was better wasted, when you're seventeen and driving you don't think about the road running out."

These lyrics will very much hit home when you've lived a few years! Dreams were there for chasing. I believe God put dreams in each of our hearts, which is why we must chase after them, but keep God first.

Go to Matthew 6:33: "_____ the _____ of _____ above all else, and _____, and He will _____ you _____ you _____." One great promise!

This promise simply means to seek God first, no matter what circumstances hit us. It means to fill our thoughts with His desires, to use His character as your life's pattern, and to keep implementing His Kingdom values on earth.

These are all lines in this song. I have to tell you I go back to my earlier days when I hear this song. Music has the ability to take us back, which is why lyrics of a song can get in our minds. It's very important to be careful with this. I am not advocating you to only listen to Christian music (as I can attest, I still do listen to "some" secular music), but be careful what you listen to. It matters! We have already established that music has the ability to alter our mood, our thoughts, emotions, and much more. This is not a study of music, but a lot is mentioned because it's such a big part of our lives, and the Bible clearly speaks, numerous times, about singing taking place in Heaven. The whole book of Psalms is a song or poem to Heaven! Sing the Psalms to Heaven!

Okay, now that we have freedom, let's move on!

Satan used a sincere motive to tempt Eve, telling her she would be like God if she ate the fruit. It wasn't wrong of Eve to want to look like God. To become more like God is humanity's highest goal.

But to become like God is not the same as trying to "be God." Our own God! We are called to reflect His characteristics and recognize His authority over our lives.

We looked at lots of Scripture today. Close by asking God in prayer to open your eyes to where you are trying to be your "own God" in your life. We ALL have those moments, but the previous passages tell us to seek His Kingdom first! Do that now. Journal some thoughts below.

Day 5

*W*ow, I have to go ahead and put this here. When God first put this study in my heart in February 2024, listening to the Grammy Awards, which I usually don't even watch, I never thought I would even have it in me. Satan, of course, put the ALL-famous question in my mind, "Did God really say?" "You don't know how to write, you've never done anything like that, etc." You know those thoughts and questions he gets us with. BUT GOD! Here we are on day 5 of week 4, with no end in sight yet. God just keeps impressing Scripture in my mind to be added, so buckle up. You've come this far; don't stop now. We are just now getting good!

So, we have established this week that salvation is the free gift of God. We didn't do anything to earn it! That even in our sin, He came to us! That through faith alone, we get the identity of "not guilty." Running around the room again is great exercise! We learned on day 2 that, in return for that free gift, there are some "expectations" for us to follow (Ephesians 4:12). Also, our response should always be praise and thanksgiving. To seek first His Kingdom, and all else we need will be added! We learned how God made Adam and Eve, the first humans, how He put it to Adam, to even NAME the animals and birds. This wrecked my mind this week!

We've established once again where sin first started and disobedience started. Now let's look at some consequences of sin and disobedience, because now Satan has planted the doubt of God's goodness in Eve's mind and convinced her to eat the fruit, and now she has also convinced Adam to eat it as well. Today we will look at Genesis 3:8. This is of course after Adam and Eve partook of the fruit on the forbidden tree.

It says: "When the cool evening breezes were blowing, the man and his wife heard the Lord God walking about in the garden. So they _____ from the Lord God among the trees. Covered themselves up with trees." Do you get the same image in your head that I get in mine when I think of this? Hide from the Lord!

The thought of this: two humans God had just made this beautiful garden for and gave them ONE tree they could not eat from, and what did they do? Yes, they disobeyed! Now, let's not put too much pressure and judgment on them. What do you think you would have done? How many times have we disobeyed? And how could they be so silly to try to hide it? Why do you think, in Genesis 3:8-11, God asked Adam and Eve these questions?

Do you think a BIG, ALL-KNOWING GOD didn't know the answers to these questions?

Yet, we do the same thing, acting as though God doesn't know what we are doing! Have the courage TODAY to share ALL you do, and the sin you may be struggling with before God. Our sin is our problem, and we can't see it because of our pride. What is your "fig leaf" today? Don't hide it from God any longer. Hiding our sin from God hinders our relationship with Him and keeps us from strengthening our relationship with Him. Think about what sin is keeping you from moving on, not allowing a closeness with God. Confess it to Him today.

Read all of Genesis 3 today, a chapter of the Bible that is often not referred to enough in society today. It's in chapter 3 we learn the consequences of Adam and Eve's disobedience. In Genesis 3:11-13, Adam and Eve played the "blame game." How often do we do that? By blaming someone else for our sin? Adam and Eve chose their course of action, as did we! That is why we sin today! But GOD … He knows the truth, and He holds EACH of us responsible for what we do (see 3:14-19). Don't try to get away with sin by shifting the blame on someone else. We are responsible for our own actions, our own decisions, and we must suffer the consequences of our own sin.

In chapter 3 of Genesis we learn that God hates sin and that He will punish sin. We also learn that disobedience is sin and breaks our fellowship with God.

We also learned that Satan is our enemy here in chapter 3. That he wants to create an atmosphere for you to linger in TEMPTATION just long enough for you to sin. And that he will do everything he can to get you to "follow" him down his deadly path. Go back to day 4 and recount the deadly Ds.

We learned here that God made our very first parents, Adam and Eve, and we are a byproduct of that!

Once again, BUT GOD …

Go over to Colossians 2:12-15. It reads: "For _____
you _____ the mighty power of God, who raised Christ
_____. You were _____ because of your _____
and because your sinful nature was not yet _____ away. Then
God made _____ alive with Christ, for he _____ ALL
our sins. He _____ the record of the charges against us and
_____ it away by _____ it to the _____."

This lets us know that, before we believed in Christ, we disobeyed,
rebelled, and ignored God, that even at our best we did not love
Him with all our hearts, souls, and minds. Every "Christian,"
however, has a NEW nature. And thank God the mortal penalty
of sin was REMOVED when Christ died on the CROSS!

Run the room, sing songs to Him, do whatever you have to do
today to get rid of sin in your life, uncover the "fig leaves" in your
life as we move into week 5 with who God says we are in Him.
Go listen to "I Got Saved." The Mt. Pisgah praise team sings this
one heavenly!

What sin are
you hiding behind a

FIG LEAF

today?

Week 5

Day 1

We are going to begin this week taking a look at our true identity in Christ. We have learned so far that we became "Christians" through God's unmerited grace, not as a result of any effort, ability, intelligent choice, or act of service on our own part. Out of gratitude for this "free gift" our hearts should overflow with a desire to help and serve others with kindness, love, and gentleness, all fruits of the Spirit (week 2).

Let's go to 2 Corinthians 5:17-21 (NLT).

This means that _____ who belongs to Christ has _____ a _____ _____. The old life is _____ ; a new life has begun. And ALL of this is a _____, who brought us back to himself _____ Christ. And God has given us this task of _____ people to him. For God was in _____, reconciling the world to himself, no longer _____ people's _____ against them. And he gave us this _____ of _____ .

Here we receive our first identity. Verse 20: "So _____ _____ Christ's _____; God is making his appeal

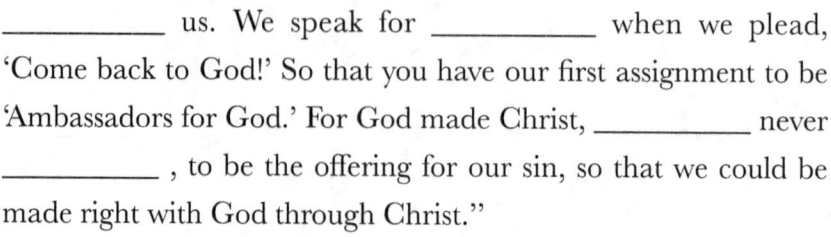

_____ us. We speak for _____ when we plead, 'Come back to God!' So that you have our first assignment to be 'Ambassadors for God.' For God made Christ, _____ never _____ , to be the offering for our sin, so that we could be made right with God through Christ."

This tells us that we don't merely turn over a new leaf, but we begin a NEW LIFE under a new master. This requires us to look at ourselves in a new light, a new perspective, a new spirit. It requires us to look at ourselves and others in a different way. God has brought us to Him, blotching out our sins, making us new IN HIM.

When we trust in Christ, we are no longer God's enemies, strangers, or foreigners. We are reconciled to Him and have the privilege of being "His Ambassadors."

What is an ambassador? Well, I'm glad you asked. Let's define this word.

An ambassador is an official representative on behalf of one country to another. As believers, we are Christ ambassadors, sent to tell the world that we can be united with Him in peace. We are His spokesperson. Remember earlier in the study we learned we are created in His image, and Ephesians 2:10 tells us we are His masterpiece created for His purposes. This is our first assignment, to represent Him in all we do.

This assignment should be one we dare not take lightly. Now we all know we are under God's grace when we sin. But ponder these questions right now:

Does your life reflect this new perspective? List ways below you think your "new life" does.

_____

_____

_____

How well are you fulfilling your commission as a "Christ Ambassador"?

_____

_____

_____

Close in prayer today, asking God how you can "shine" in your new role.

Find the Casting Crowns song, "God of All My Days." Worship Him through this song today!

Day 2

hat was a heavy task assigned to us in yesterday's lesson. I guess you were asking yourself, "How can I do this?" I know I was when I first became a Christian. That was the first question I had for myself: What does Christianity look like? What do I do next? How? When? Why? Where? All of the tough questions!

The answer to this overwhelming question is, "You can't." Sorry to knock the breath out of you, but that's the reality—that we are "not enough" to do this alone. That we can only do this through Him and His strength.

Romans 7:18 says this: "And I know that nothing good lives in me, that is, in my sinful nature. I want to do what is right, but I can't."

This tells us that we have the right mindset, but we can't do it on our own.

Go and read the rest of Romans 7:19-24. What does it say? Right—that you can't. BUT GOD …

Now look at verse 25: "THANK GOD! The _____ is in _____ our Lord. So you see how it is: In _____ I really

want to _____ God's law, but because of my _____
I am a slave to sin."

So you see, we can't, but GOD CAN through us.

Romans 8:1 tells us there is no condemnation for those who belong
to Christ Jesus. And 8:2 says this: "And because _____
belong to _____, the _____ of the life giving Spirit
has _____ you from the power of sin that _____ to
_____."

Here it is: this means the power within you, the Holy Spirit, the
third person of the trinity, gives us the power we need to live the
Christian life. That Jesus gave His life for us so that we might receive
the power of the Holy Spirit.

Stop trying to live in your own strength; you can't. I can't, none
of us can, your pastor can't, your parents can't, your grandparents
can't. We just can't do it. The Bible mentions the word "strength"
360 times, and it is often linked to God's power. We could list verse
after verse about His strength and how He is our strength.

If you feel low in strength today, look up your favorite verse and
pray it today! Psalms 119:27-28 says this: "Help me to understand
the meaning of your commandments, and I will meditate on your
wonderful deeds. I weep with sorrow; encourage me by your word."

Life is cluttered with how-to books and self-help books, but the
authors of those books can't come alongside each of us to help us
follow those directions.

BUT GOD ... does with His book, the Bible. This is the unique-
ness of the Bible. God not only provides the rules and guidelines but

also comes with us personally each day, through the Holy Spirit, to strengthen us so that we can live according to those guidelines. All we have to do is invite Him to and then respond to His direction.

Ask Him in prayer today what direction He may be leading you into.

Go listen to Jamie Grace's songs "You Lead" and "Do Life Big." These two songs give us lyrics that let God lead and us follow!

You simply cannot please God without faith. The need for "security" and "comfort" LIMITS the ability of God to move in your life.

Day 3

We are going to be going into more of what God's Word says about "who we are" and "what we were made for," but before we do I am trying to establish some guidelines on how the Bible tells us to live in a fallen world, as "redeemed" people.

Let's look at Romans 12:1: "And so, dear _____ and _____ I _____ with you to give your _____ to God because of ALL _____ has done for _____. Let them be a living and holy sacrifice—the kind He will find _____. This is truly the way to _____ him."

What does this say? How do we do this?

_____

_____

_____

God has good, pleasing, perfect plans for us (Jeremiah 29:11). He wants us to be transformed people with renewed minds living to honor and obey Him and to serve others in the name of Jesus. We must joyfully "give" ourselves to Him daily!

Now Romans 12:2: "Don't _____ the behavior and _____ of this _____, but let _____ transform _____ into a _____ person by _____ the way _____ think. Then you will learn to _____ God's will for _____, which is _____ and _____ and _____ ."

What does this verse mean to you? How do you go deeper with God and move away from the world and the world views?

_____

_____

_____

Our refusal to conform to this world must go deeper than just our behavior and customs. It must be firmly planted in the values rooted in our minds. We have to let God transform us into a new person by the way we think. Only when the Holy Spirit renews, reeducates, and redirects our minds are we truly transformed!

Turn over to Romans 8:5-6: "Those who are dominated by the sinful nature think about sinful things, but those who are controlled by the Holy Spirit think about things that please the Spirit. So letting your sinful nature control your mind leads to death."

What is Paul saying in these two verses?

_____

_____

_____

Here Paul divides us into two categories: those who are dominated by their sinful nature and those who are controlled by the Holy Spirit. All of us would be in the first category if Jesus hadn't offered us a way out. We must choose daily to renew our minds and follow Him. According to Wikipedia the phrase "What would Jesus do?", often shortened to WWJD, became popular particularly in the US in the early 1900s after the widely read book *In His Steps: What Would Jesus Do?* by Charles Sheldon.

The resurgence of the motto during the 1990s stems from the WWJD abbreviation on wristbands that became popular among Christian youth groups.

So here you have it. We must renew our minds daily and ask ourselves WWJD in ALL situations. And this will be acceptable to God according to His Word.

Wrap up today asking yourself how you can do this and how you can respond to all situations in a fallen, sinful world. Stay tuned tomorrow for more on how to not be conformed to this world and its sin. We don't do it alone!

Go listen to "No Longer Slaves." Bethel Music is my favorite on this one! Enjoy!

Day 4

*I*n continuing our study on how to live in a sin-fallen world, I want us to look today at Romans 8:26-30. Most people have taken a good hard look at this "refrigerator verse," but we don't look at the two verses that precede it and the two verses that follow it. Before we go any further let's define "refrigerator verses." Those are very common verses of Scripture that you may see on a magnet for a refrigerator or a sign hanging in a store, maybe even in your own home. These are verses that even someone who may not have picked up a Bible in their lifetime may even know. Or at least they have seen them somewhere—maybe in Grandmother's home, your home, a notebook, anywhere other than the Bible.

Let's do that now. Pray now for God to open your eyes to what "thing" you are "holding" onto that you feel is "not good."

Romans 8:28 says this: "And we _____ that God causes _____ to work _____ for the _____ of those who _____ God and are _____ according to _____ for them."

Whew, that's a mouthful! God works ALL things for good? When's the last time you felt that? Paul writes here that we can know that every single thing God works for good. Think about that "thing" right now. List your "thing" you may be going through right now.

_____

_____

_____

We are living in a culture where we are told to feel "comfortable." Where our feelings are what matter most, where we have to "feel good" all the time.

Well, I hate to tell you, but in this life, we will have trials and temptations. Read the whole book of James; he will step on your toes a little!

If you are trying to find "comfort" in your "things," whatever they may be—death, breakup, divorce, child loss, child estrangement, broken friendships, health diagnoses—our list of "things" could go on and on. BUT GOD ...

We must believe that since we are a new creation, being used for God's purposes, that God works in ALL things, not just the "good" or "comfortable" things. We have to believe that, even though evil pervades our fallen world, God is able to turn every circumstance around for our long-range benefit. We must note that God is not working to make US HAPPY but to fulfill His purposes.

Let's read on to verse 29: "For God _____ his people in advance, and he _____ them to become like his _____, so that His Son would be the _____ among many brothers and sisters."

What is this verse saying? Thoughts? Now lots of people have lots to say about this verse. Some people think that certain people were destined by God ahead of time to come to Him; others believe that God only chose certain people to give His free gift of salvation to. And I am not here to debate this verse. I want you to get what is stuck right in the middle of this verse, which is what?

To become more like who? _____

Yes, His Son! God's ultimate goal for us is to make us more in the image of His Son. Since we are made in the image of His Son, what do you think we may have to endure? Do you think Jesus had to endure pain and suffering? List some thoughts.

_____

_____

_____

Let's close today thanking Him for who He is and what He's done for us in ALL things! 1 Thessalonians 5:18 says this: "In EVERY situation, be thankful and continually give thanks to God; for this is the will of God for you in Christ Jesus." Amen. You pick your favorite worship song today! Have fun singing praises to Him!

Day 5

As promised on day 3, this week we are going to take a look at how we can live and carry on in a sin-stricken world and this thing we call life.

List ways that you think you can "get by" in this world:

_____

_____

_____

Now let's turn again to Romans 8:26-27: "And the _____ _____ _____ us in our _____. For example, we don't know what God wants us to _____ for. But the _____ prays for us with groanings that _____ be expressed in words. And the Father who _____ ALL hearts knows what the Spirit is saying, for the Spirit pleads for _____ believers [Greek for "God's holy people"] in _____ with God's own _____ ."

What does this verse mean? What is it saying?

It is saying that, as believers, we are not left to our own resources to cope with problems. Even when you don't know what to pray, tell the Holy Spirit to pray God's will for you—to intercede for you. Then TRUST that He will always do what's best for you!

I want to stop and say this right here—lots of times, when we are going through hard times, someone, even a nonbeliever, may ask us this question, "As a Christian do you not believe God works All things for good?" We learned yesterday what "refrigerator verses" are and that even non-Christians may have seen them somewhere.

But they have never opened a Bible to read the two preceding verses, and as Christians we are called to read and believe All verses, not just the ones we may know or see regularly somewhere! This is why we have to stay prayed up and know Scripture, so this person in front of you gets to hear "why" we believe what we say we do!

Let's read a few more verses today that stand out about how God stands for us.

Read all of Romans 8:31-38 and answer the following questions after reading.

Do you ever think that, because you aren't good enough for God, He will not "save" you? Verses 31-34 tell us differently. If you have reached this point in the Bible study and are still questioning your salvation, my prayer is that you speak with someone today about salvation. A pastor or church leader would love to talk with you. Seek them today!

If God is for us, who could be against us?

Can anything separate you from God's love?

These verses contain some of the most "comforting" promises in all the Bible.

Look up your favorite promise in the Bible, and pray it today for yourself or your loved one! Close in prayer, thanking Him for this promise or promises. Use the space below to journal it.

_____

_____

_____

A Letter on the Youth

In this section of the Bible study, we will take a look over some statistics on youth and the mental health crisis, as well as the tactics the enemy, walking around seeing whom he may devour next, is using against our youth. Now, I know that God has a plan for this generation, and I believe that this will be the generation that God will use to "change the world." I am by no means a professional on youth and make no claims that I have them figured out! The Lord called me to serve youth in my church three years ago, in August 2021. I remember the literal "terror" that I felt that first August evening as I stepped back into the youth area, complete with a "hang out" area, worship area, pizza, drinks, games, all things that scream youth! Smoke machines and all! I had just "retired" from my job of thirty-nine years. I had managed several different age groups, including a lot of sixteen-year-olds, legal job age. This was a much different thing though. I knew beyond a shadow of a doubt that this was what the Lord had for me during this season of my life, but I still questioned, "Did God really say?" After about six months, I was still asking the same question, but I continued praying that God would give me the wisdom to teach and help instruct these young ladies in the ways of the Lord.

The youth pastor assured me I could do this, and I still questioned whether or not he or I, either one, actually heard from the Lord. Just kidding! I had so many confirmations about this decision, and I knew that had I not taken this step of faith, I would have been in disobedience!

Keep in mind, youth groups usually serve sixth through twelfth graders. Take a guess which group I was given? Yup, you got it: sixth graders. Whew, I haven't had a sixth grader in twenty-nine years. I only ever raised one daughter, who at this time was thirty-seven years old.

There were tears of joy, tears of sorrow, and any other tears you may want to add here. If you've ever been around a group of sixth graders, you are sure to know, there is ALWAYS drama. My worst pet peeve. Drama. I can't tell you how many times I asked God the question, "Did you really say for me to come back here?" Then another pastor in the church came and asked me to teach the middle school group class, much like Sunday School. This now included sixth through eighth graders. Well, let's just go ahead and make a long story short (because I have plenty of them). Three years later, I am still there serving youth girls, and I LOVE it. I believe that I will see some of these young ladies change the world, and I can't wait to see it!

The mandate of Titus 2:3-5 is that older women are to discipline younger women, teaching them how to grow in godliness in their distinct relationships and calling. There you have it: the church is responsible to encourage and equip women to disciple each other. For now, I will continue to serve in youth ministry until the Lord calls me into something different or directs me in another direction.

I have a strong desire to help girls and women see through God's Word to find "who they are" and "whose they are." I feel they can change the world once they grab hold of the truths of God's Word about how they are designed and their purpose.

Two words that seem to have fueled the world's understanding of women in culture in recent decades: girl power. Female empowerment is, at its core, about helping girls and women recognize their worth. Seems innocent enough, right? If only it were that simple. It's apparent that Christian mothers and girls today are at a crossroads. How can girls and women advocate for "girl power" when the feminist movement in America is tied to so many activities and beliefs that oppose Christian values?

Embracing the concepts behind "pioneer girls"—the two words I have for them—is impossible you say, right? I believe it doesn't have to be. Why? The current "girl power" movement places all its meaning in the human understanding of man and woman, embracing concepts of cultural feminism as the sole source of worth. But we know as Christians that humankind's purpose doesn't come from Earthly sources—it's of God. Just as worth does not come from intelligence, appearance, or wealth, nor does it come from the idea of feminine validation. I believe that, while submitting themselves to an almighty God, they will see that God's power is in all things. I believe that together, girls and their mothers and their adult leaders can embrace the "pioneer girls" movement, not out of a place of "entitlement" but rather in a light of grace from the Lord. I believe raising girls in an environment of strong faith and wide-spanning opportunity will grow them into confident women of integrity. My prayer is for these young ladies to recognize their worth and identity in Christ. The full value and strength of a woman is only understood through the lens of Christ. As with any question, one can turn to His Word for clarity and guidance toward understanding. (The pioneer spirit will be further detailed in the closing statement of this book.)

My prayer for you through the coming weeks, and the rest of your life, is this:

> Ephesians 3:16-19 (NIV): "I pray that out of his glorious riches he may strengthen you with power through his Spirit in your inner being, so that Christ may dwell in your hearts through faith. And I pray that you, being rooted and established in love, may have power, together with all the Lord's holy people, to grasp how wide and long and how high and deep is the love of Christ, and to know this love that surpasses knowledge—that you may be filled to the measure of ALL the fullness of God."

A girl's mission in life not only includes the many accomplishments she's sure to achieve but also the great joy in offering up her life's success in praise to God. What a calling that is!

Over the summer of 2024, I attended a youth camp with my church. We had breakout sessions, and in one of our sessions a young lady who had been dealing with depression and anxiety had the following statistics. (This was such a God wink as I was researching this about the time of this camp and had also gotten some statistics from a documentary on Netflix called *The Social Dilemma*.) The fact of the matter is, although we have a world of information at our fingertips, which information is true and correct? This is why I chose to not sift through a lot of different websites, which becomes very overwhelming, and instead chose to use some statistics from what I hope are reliable sources. You can do your own research and find that. But my point here is this, these teens are facing some unprecedented challenges, and they need to know their worth and identity in Christ at a much earlier age than ever before, I believe.

According to the Anxiety and Depression Association of America, "Anxiety disorders affect 31.9% of adolescents between the ages of 13 and 18 years old."

A study published by the American Academy of Pediatrics reports that between January 2016 and December 2022 for individuals between the ages of 12 and 25, the monthly antidepressant dispensing rate increased 66.3%.

In 2021, 42% of adolescents reported feeling sad or hopeless. Does this figure not astound you?

On October 19, 2021, the American Academy of Pediatrics, the American Academy of Child and Adolescent Psychiatry, and the Children's Hospital Association declared a national emergency of mental health issues in children and adolescents.

In the documentary *The Social Dilemma* on Netflix, Jonathan Haidt, PHD, NYU Stern School of Business, Social Psychologist, listed the following statistics.

The number has increased greatly with teenage girls in depression and anxiety. His chart shows that until 2010 hospital admissions were pretty stable.

Then between 2011-2013 the number of teenage girls admitted to a hospital for cutting or other means of self-harm was up 62% for older teen girls (ages 15-19) and up 189% for preteen girls (ages 10-14). This is nearly triple.

US suicide rates compared to an average from 2001-2010: girls age 10-14, up 151%; girls aged 15-19, up 70%.

If you are reading this and have suicidal thoughts, or know someone who does, the suicide hotline number is 988. Make the call today or make the call to a friend, a parent, a church leader, someone, anyone. A pastor of your local church would love to talk to you. Make that call.

The National Center for Drug Abuse Statistics has the following findings.

Youth drug abuse is a high-profile public health concern, with at least one in eight teenagers abusing an illicit substance in the last year.

The key findings listed on their website on August 5, 2024, were as follows:

- Drug use went up 61% among eighth graders between 2016 and 2020.
- 62% of teenagers in twelfth grade have abused alcohol.
- 2.08 million or 8.33% of twelve-to seventeen-year-olds nationwide report using drugs in the last month; among them 83.88% reported having used marijuana in the last month.
- 8.7% of eighth graders have used illicit drugs other than marijuana in the last month.
- 21.3 percent of eighth graders have tried illicit drugs in the last month.
- By the time they're in twelfth grade, 46.6% of teens have tried illicit drugs.
- 4,777 Americans aged fourteen to twenty-four years old died of an overdose of illicit drugs in one year. (This number

will continue to rise with the opioid crisis. And the rate of fentanyl is taking over the US.)

- Early drug abuse correlates with substance abuse problems later in life, and the most significant increases in destructive behavior appear to take place among older teens and young adults.
- Opioid abuse is considered a national public health emergency.
- Overdose deaths due to opioids have increased 500% among fifteen-to twenty-four-year-olds since 1999.
- In the twenty-first century, opioid-related OD deaths among this age group increased by as much as 30.7% annually.
- High school students who legitimately use prescription opioids are 33% more likely to misuse opioids after high school.
- 5.3% of twelfth graders have abused opioids other than heroin at least once.
- In the past year, 2.4% of twelfth graders abused OxyContin while 1.2% abused Vicodin.

If you or someone you know is dealing with drug or alcohol abuse, there are several resources local to your town. Please seek help today!

There are several facilities in your area that are willing to meet you where you are. Reach out to one today, or call the crisis hotline at 988, and you will be directed to one in your area. Or go to a local church. They would be glad to offer local resources. Don't wait, do it now.

Youth Alcohol Abuse

Alcohol is by far the most commonly abused substance among teens and young adults.

- 1.19 million twelve-to seventeen-year-olds report binge drinking in the last month.
- 25.6% of eighth graders have abused alcohol at least once.
- 61.5% of teens have abused alcohol by twelfth grade.
- 407,000 teenagers aged twelve to seventeen years old met the criteria for alcohol use disorder (AUD) in the last year.
- In the state of South Carolina 8.11% of teens use drugs and 8.89% use alcohol.

Teen Sex

Oh boy is this a wide-open topic, whew!

I am just going to list this from the CDC National Center for Health Statistics (June 22, 2017).

An estimated 55% of male and female teens have had sexual intercourse by age eighteen, and approximately 80% of teens used some form of contraception at first sex.

There are so many different websites, all giving their ideas on teen sex and the education of the topic. I learned during my own research that you need to do your own deep dive, making ABSOLUTE sure you note who the researchers are and who is funding the research. Only twenty-two US states require that, if provided, sex education must be medically, factually, or technically accurate. This leaves a lot of room for misinformation and also information that you may not deem moral. In doing this research I spent a lot of time going to different articles, and I just want to put this out there. One article I came across had some great statistics and what I felt to be true and correct about teen sex and pregnancy. The more I read the article, I started to realize that some of the thoughts that the writer was listing did not line up biblically. After going back to who wrote the article, I realized that this lady was part of the LGBTQ community and writing for planned parenthood. No, I DON'T NEED YOUR EDUCATION. We don't have the same views and opinions on God's design for our bodies. Be careful what you see little eyes!

Among the mental health crisis for teens is the pressure of "sexting." Sexting is defined as sending sexually explicit messages, photos, or video via cell phone, computer, or any digital device. This is a topic that all teens and parents need heavy education on. True education. This can become a case of cyberbullying, which leads to mental health in general. I believe this is one of the main reasons that teen suicide rates are up. Many teens are being lured to send nude photos, and unfortunately many don't understand the lifelong consequences that sharing explicit photos can have on their lives. This bullying on sexting, believe it or not, is happening more among the males than females.

If you are in Greenville, South Carolina, Switch, a local human trafficking organization, is leading a movement to end human sex trafficking and sexual exploitation. I actually served with this ministry for six years, and I know this is a faith-based ministry, serving the upstate with great intentions. They have a great prevention program for youth, led by some amazing folks! They have a separate educational seminar on "sexting." For more information, go online to: Switchsc.org. You can request a speaker online or call for more information.

This is an age-appropriate topic and should be discussed with your parents. But I do want to also add here that I have had girls as young as sixth grade admit to sexting. I just want to also add that the Bible, the truth, has a lot to say on God's design for sex and marriage. Again, here we are with what could be another full Bible study. I am just trying to get the point across that all of these life topics are being discussed as early as fourth grade.

I want to elaborate on that for a few minutes. I volunteered in an elementary school starting in the fall of the 2023-2024 school year. During this time, I stayed three hours, twice a month, so six hours a month. While I wasn't surprised, I was really saddened by some of the stories I heard during this time. I will tell you that if you are not educating your kids at home, the right education, they are getting it at school. Some children are in home lives that you may have never imagined. I believe the Lord gave me this opportunity to let me see that, in my own personal journey of growing up (to be another book soon), I wasn't the only kid who had seen some unwanted "stuff," and not everyone grows up in church and has biblical teaching at home. God opened my eyes, even more, through the eyes of a little five-year-old girl, who I will just say I had gotten attached to. One day she came into the lunch room very upset and teared up telling me she was moving, and she would never see me again. I responded with, "I will be praying for you, and God will take care of you." She responded, "What is prayer, and who is that?" Now I am in a public school setting and a volunteer; keep that in mind. I can't be fired for speaking on this topic! Can you believe that this cafeteria that I served in is less than four miles from my church and a mile away from a local community church, and this little girl had never heard of God or prayer? Ponder that!

If you are a teen reader and find yourself pregnant and feel you have no one to talk to, there is a national teen pregnancy number for you to call and talk to someone. The number is 1-800-672-2296. This number should not take the place of a parent or guardian. And if you feel like you can't talk to them at this time, try talking to a youth leader in a local church. They would love to talk with you and help you find resources and pray with you.

During the coming weeks of the study there may be a time when you feel like this study is stepping on your toes; hear my heart here, please. This study has nothing to do with me being any different than you on emotions and what to do with them. Mental health is a touchy subject among Christians today. I am not putting any opinions from any articles that I've read, any books that I've read, because the topic of faith versus feeling is a broad controversial topic. I will say if you are being seen by a mental health specialist, the next few weeks of study COULD be something different than what you may have heard from him or her. With that in mind, please keep in mind I AM NOT a medical professional, and I am not pointing you away from one, nor am I pointing you to one. I am just pointing you to the truth of God's Word and how we have the power of His Word when we are a new creation, saved by His grace, and made new. We are now new!

I want us to take a look at a couple of verses that tell us that. Read Ephesians 4:14-16.

What does this say? It says that Christ is the truth (John 14:6), and the Holy Spirit, who guides the church, is the Spirit of truth (John 16:13). Satan by contrast, is the father of lies (John 8:44). As followers of Christ, we must be committed to the truth. This means our words should be honest and our actions should reflect

Christ's integrity. To accomplish Christ's work in the world, we must ALWAYS speak the truth in love, no matter how difficult, inconvenient, or unpleasant.

I believe we should have childlike faith, but we should test ideas with full-grown discernment.

In the era of social media, internet, self-help books, personality tests, etc., there is a lot out there competing for our attention, all kinds of ways to get us side-tracked. But ultimately, we must bring it back to Scripture and what we as Christians believe!

Week 6

*N*ow that you have read some statistics on youth, I hope you have heard my heart on youth and the mental health crisis that is factual. I want to introduce you to my thoughts on emotions and feelings, but most importantly I will take you to the Word of God in week 6 to show you passages from God's Word that I feel, if grabbed hold of, could put a dent in the current teen mental health crisis. I am NOT a medical professional, and know that I am in no way trying to "unsettle" what a medical professional may have told you on mental health. I just simply will be stating what God's Word directs us to do when we get into our feelings and emotions.

The world tells us we have to "feel" good all the time. It won't happen. We are designed in God's image (Genesis 1:27). The shortest verse in the English-language Bible is John 11:35: "Jesus wept." Yes, Jesus had feelings and emotions also. We are going to feel and have emotions, but it is how we react to them that matters most. As believers and Christians, we are called to react with the fruit of the Spirit. Will we do it at all times? No, I don't believe we will. But we must strive to not let our feelings and emotions overtake us and have self-control. I do believe we live in a "the devil made me do it" kind of world and should own more of our actions or should I say reactions to our feelings. Feelings have a very big role in how we live out our lives, and we could do another whole study on that, but I want us to stick to what this study is written for—our identity in Christ. Once we know this, your life will CHANGE, and your relationships will look a lot different. I pray that, through the next few weeks, you learn how to guard your heart and mind and allow God to show you, through His Word, how to respond and control your emotions.

The three I's of Scripture are: Inspired, meaning that God is the definitive author; Inerrant, meaning God used human authors to pen exactly what God wanted, without any mixture of error; and Infallible, meaning God's Word is incapable of error.

Christians use a lot of words to describe what they believe about the Bible. But if you're new to the faith, or you haven't grown up around the church (like myself), these words can be a little confusing.

2 Peter 1:3 says that "God has provided ALL we need for life and godliness through Christ Jesus." He is enough; in Him you are enough. Happy studying! Prayers for you as you go through the next three weeks!

I want to introduce you to the song lyrics of the song God used to bring this Bible study to life through me. It is a song that continually tells us she doesn't know how to "feel." We all have emotions and feelings, and we will see later through God's Word that He does as well!

Did you see the *Barbie* movie? I typically am not a fan of Disney movies, so I don't go to them. Music has ALWAYS been my favorite, not movies. I did watch this, as I needed to understand the song, "What Was I Made For?" and how it related to the movie. Remember, Billie Eilish wrote this song specifically for the movie and won "Song of the Year" at the 66th Annual Grammy Awards in February 2024. I almost already knew, by the lines of the song, the meaning behind it, but I had to be sure! As noted, music plays a big role in most of our lives and can change the mood, mindset, and so much more by listening to it. We really can get to a place of believing the lyrics of songs, as music is written by what someone "feels."

I am not going to dissect the movie, but if you have not seen it, it is a movie where Barbie finds herself losing her grip over her inherent Barbie-ness. She and Ken both question their identity, and in one part of the movie, Barbie gets to go to the "real world" so that she can know "the truth about the universe." This in return leads her, at the end of the movie, to go to her maker, Ruth Handler, and ask the question, "What was I made for?" At this time her maker starts to speak to her on this matter, and Barbie decides that the best option for her is to go back to the "real world" instead of Barbie land.

Here we are in the "real world." Yes, Barbie, it's hard. It can be tough at times. We have feelings, we have emotions and "stuff" that we all have to go through and deal with. I want us to see in the coming weeks how God's Word tells us who we are and what we are made for. His Word also gives us HOPE in such a sin-corrupted world. We can fall in a place in our minds where we curse the darkness and forget that we are called to be "the Light" in the darkness (Matthew 5:14). God knew the world was going to be dark, and yet He placed us here, right in the middle "for such a time as this" (Esther 4:14). I want us to see that God can, will, and does use "everything" in our lives to grow us more into His image. He uses all the broken pieces, and nothing is wasted!

The lyrics of the song "What Was I Made For?" begin with Barbie questioning how she's starting to change and beginning to question her place in the world. "I used to float, now I just fall down, I used to know, but I'm not sure now. What was I made for? Takin a drive, I was an ideal. Looked so alive, turns out, I'm not real. Just something you paid for. What was I made for?"

However, by the time you get to the chorus of the song Barbie expresses her desire to someday understand her feelings: "Cause I don't know how to feel, but someday I might."

How many times has a song made you "feel" some kind of way? Lonely, sad, depressed, happy, motivated… Yes, we can get into ALL of our emotions when we are listening to music.

The song goes on to say, "Think I forgot how to be happy. Something I'm not, but something I can be."

The lyrics here deceive us into thinking we need to be "happy." Happiness doesn't come from the world; if we are seeking happiness in the world, this is our first mistake. The Bible says the Joy of the Lord is my strength (Nehemiah 8:10).

Joy and happiness are two different things. Boy, was this statement a hard one for me to learn.

In verse 3 of the song, she asks herself, "When did it end? All the enjoyment. I'm sad again, don't tell my boyfriend. It's not what he's made for. What was I made for?"

I hope through the next couple of weeks, you learn through God's Word "how to be happy," how when you are in your feelings or emotions, you take them to God first, not your boyfriend. No, this is not what he was made for, nor you!

It continues with, "Think I forgot how to be happy. Something I'm not, but something I can be. Something I wait for, something I'm made for. Something I'm made for. I don't know how to feel, but I wanna try. I don't know how to feel, but someday, I might. Someday I might."

Here we are "waiting" on our happiness, because one day it might come. Barbie is just a hot mess in this movie, and she gets into her feelings and talks herself into waiting to be "happy." We don't have to wait for "happiness" till it just suddenly appears, and if I can let you in on my little secret, it doesn't just happen to appear one day! We are repeatedly told throughout Scripture to "Rejoice in the Lord always" (Philippians 4:4). To give thanks for the blessing of God's grace and mercy. And that true happiness comes from our faith and love for God. The happiness of this world is fleeting and superficial compared to the joy of everlasting life by faith in Jesus Christ!

On January 12, 2024, Josh Baldwin dropped his single, and title track, from his solo album, "Made for More." Just six months earlier, and a whole different genre of music, Billie Eilish released the song, "What Was I Made For?" (the inspiration for this study).

Josh Baldwin's song is definitely an answer to the question, "What Was I Made For?" "Made for More" became my "theme song" for this study. One of the ways the Lord confirmed this study was through our youth camp. Our youth camp theme this year was "Made For More." I have listened to this song so many times, I could likely sing it in my sleep! (You might not want to hear that!) The lyrics of this song tell us we are "Made for More."

If you haven't heard this amazing song, go listen to it now! (Put it on repeat!)

"You weren't made to be tending a grave." This song screams the truth of Scripture on why you were made, who you are in Christ, a new creation. It makes me want to RUN. Once you grab this truth, the other stuff all falls into place. Go for a walk in nature and find peace before jumping on this week's emotional roller coaster! Get ready!

All my love,
Mary Ann

Day 1

Remember in the Billie Eilish song "What Was I Made For?" she says, "I don't know how to feel."

Once again, we live in a world where we are being told to go to self-help classes or yoga classes, read books, or even take medication to tell us how to feel. The world tells us to "look inward" and "be who you want to be," among other "selfie identities." Remember, we live in a selfie world!

The Bible tells us that, if we look inward, all our righteousness are filthy rags (Isaiah 64:6). We are ridden with sin; that's the world we were born into. Romans 5:12 says, "Just as sin entered the world through one man, and death through sin, and in this way, death came to all people, because all sinned."

Now 1 John 1:9 says, "If we confess our sins, he is faithful and just to forgive us our sins, and to cleanse us from all unrighteousness." If you have not yet received the free gift of salvation, today is the day. Talk to a pastor at your local church; they would LOVE to sit down and talk to you about salvation.

I don't want to sound insensitive here, and if you are seeking a medical professional for mental health, please hear my heart, and know that I am just pointing out the truths of Scripture here. And by no means am I saying that mental health is not important. But what I am saying is this: the world is going to point you in a different direction, not into the sufficiency of Scripture. Turn to 2 Timothy 3:16-17. What does it say? Yes, that "ALL scripture is inspired by God and profitable for teaching, for reproof, for correction, for training in righteousness, so that the man of God may be adequate, equipped for every good work."

Yes, we do have a mental health crisis on our hands, and what should be done about it? I believe we must turn back to the ways of the Lord, because we have moved so far away from that. We could look around the world, possibly even in our own homes right now, and see what a sin-stricken world we live in. We must not, as Christians, get caught up in all the distractions going on around us. We are put here on earth for a purpose, for a plan, for such a time as this. We must be the light we are called to be and not get stuck in what we could easily call our "feelings." There's a battle that we must always be fighting against the flesh, and that battle resides in our feelings. Our feelings will lead us to do what feels right or good—whether or not it is considered righteous by God. Our feelings will try to persuade us to do things that are disobedient to God. If we are to live a righteous life, they cannot be trusted.

2 Corinthians 5:7 says what?

_____

_____

_____

We are called not to live by our feelings but by faith!

Proverbs 3:5-6 says what?

_____

_____

_____

Our own understanding would be where our "feelings" are. We all have them!

What else does Paul tell us to do in Romans 12:1-2?

_____

_____

_____

Yes, it wants us to be transformed people with renewed minds, living to honor and obey Him and to serve others in the name of Jesus. Verse 2 is a warning against following the selfish and corrupt world. Only when the Holy Spirit renews, reeducates, and redirects our minds are we truly transformed. turn to Romans 8:5. What does it say? Here we are divided into two categories: those who are dominated by their sinful nature and those who are controlled by the Holy Spirit. All of us would be in the first category if Jesus hadn't offered us a way out! We learned earlier in the Bible study, in the "I Am" statements, that He is the only way. Choose for yourself today who you will follow!

Let's take a look at one command from the Word: Turn to 2 Corinthians 10:5.

What is this verse telling us?

_____

_____

_____

Now turn to Proverbs 23:7: What does this verse tell us?

_____

_____

_____

This verse tells us that our thoughts determine who we are, and the verse above that we just looked at tells us what? That we must bring every thought captive to the obedience of Christ. How do we do that?

_____

_____

_____

Does God expect us to train our feelings? It appears in Scripture that He does. He commands them.

Romans 6:17 says what?

_____

_____

_____

Here God commands our obedience. From the heart, the vessel we often judge as ungovernable.

Luke 12:4-5 says what?

_____

_____

_____

Yes, what to fear and what not to fear.

Philippians 4:4 tells us what?

_____

_____

_____

Yes, what we must and must not delight in.

Romans 12:9 says what?

_____

_____

_____

Boy, here's a command that can be found throughout Scripture. To do what? Love, yes! Most of us have learned how to be courteous to others—how to speak kindly, avoid hurting other people's feelings, and appear to take interest in them. We may even be skilled in pretending to feel compassion when we hear of others needs. But God calls us to go beyond that, far beyond pretense and politeness. He calls us to genuine love. Genuine love requires effort and concentration, and it won't come through not managing our emotions.

Philippians 4:6 tells us what?

_____

_____

_____

Ephesians 4:26 tells us what?

_____

_____

_____

When we only deal with our actions, we are left with moralism, not Christianity. Outward conformity in behavior alone is meaningless when inside we are full of emotional uncleanliness.

Now read Romans 8:26-27 What is He telling us here?

_____

_____

_____

Yes, that as a believer, you are not left to your own resources to cope with problems. This is great news: we are not left to be enslaved to our emotions.

How does He teach us to love and feel in line with godliness?

1. His Son. The person of Jesus Christ, the perfect-feeler,
    who lived the emotional life we couldn't and suffered
    the emotion-crushing wrath on our behalf, all in order
    to make us new down to the core of our emotions

(Matthew 27:46). Has there ever been a more emotionally distraught cry?

2. His Spirit. God has given us His own Spirit to produce affectional fruit pleasing to God. Galatians 5:22-23: Love (instead of hate), joy (instead of despair), peace (instead of turmoil), patience (instead of anger), kindness (instead of severity), goodness (instead of badness), faithfulness (instead of temperamentality), gentleness (instead of harshness), self-control (instead of passions-control). He addresses our emotional lives at the source: our hearts.

3. His People. God doesn't tell us to surround ourselves with self-help books, daytime talk shows, or yoga classmates to balance our emotional states. He surrounds us with His people. Sanctification, never forget, is a community project. The older instruct the younger. All serve one another with varying gifts. Hear the word, and live it together. And build each other up, "speaking the truth in love" (Ephesians 4:15).

4. And last, but definitely not least, He gives us His Word. Finally, God reveals with a capital "R" Reality through His Word to be believed by faith. Hebrews 11:1 says what? Now read Colossians 3:15-16. The peace of Christ rules in our hearts when His Word dwells richly in us.

For example, in the span of four verses, Paul points us to one aspect of Reality that, when believed, will liberate us from anxiety and impart undauntable joy. Read Philippians 4:4-7. What does it say?

He doesn't merely tell us to "sing in the Lord" or "dance in the Lord" or "smile in the Lord," but "rejoice in the Lord."

When should we rejoice? Always. When should we stop? Never! The world's reality tells us that if we are single, wronged, jilted, or oppressed, we have a right to be "unhappy." Here Paul thinks differently; he inhabits a different world. A changed man, by God's amazing grace! He is near to hear our prayers. He is near to comfort us. Nothing can separate us from His love.

Listen to the song, "It Is Well" by your favorite artist. Boy, does it have a way to wash peace over you!

Day 2

Here is where we get our "toes" stepped on. The debate over "faith" over "feelings" can be a touchy subject. I want you to hear my heart over the next couple of days and weeks. I want to go ahead and insert right here that I have not always practiced faith over feelings. Just talk to someone whom I was "boss" to when I was in my twenties. (I was always a "boss" to a team of people in restaurants.) I am now in my late fifties and can very much tell you that I was a mostly "angry" person my whole life until the year 2010, when I was saved by God's amazing grace. You see, I was raised in a home where mostly the emotion of anger was shown. The word or emotion of "love" was never mentioned or shown. So, let me say this: I was a "ticking time bomb" most of the time. I ran the restaurant not caring about anyone's feelings except my own. I had a "my way or the highway" mentality. Boy, did I go through a lot of employees with this attitude. I remember one time my anger had gotten the best of me, and I literally almost hit an employee. Thank God, I had an assistant manager at the time that demanded I go sit down in the office to "cool off."

After that day, I realized while sitting there, not a Christian at this time, that I had to take control over my emotion of anger and not let it control me. This is when I started to learn that I needed some leadership skills, and not be a "boss" but a leader. (There is a difference you know!) I had taken anger as an identity.

How many men and women do you think are sitting in a prison cell today, wishing they had taken control over their rage and anger before they picked up the gun and shot someone? Or beat someone to death in a rage? In these instances, we have allowed our emotions to take over, and our reasoning shuts down. I could very well be the one sitting in a prison cell waiting for my time to be up or possibly for my life. But thank God my reasoning kicked in that day and took over my anger.

I tell you that story to let you know that I have NOT always used faith over my feelings and emotions, and sometimes I still struggle with it today, even as a Christian. Because, after all, we do still wrestle against the flesh. Remember back in week 2, day 3 of this study on putting on "The Armor of God." Ephesians 6:12 tells us that.

None of us have "arrived," and ALL of us struggle with feelings and emotions.

Let's first define feelings and emotions.

Webster defines "feelings" as an emotional state or reaction: "a feeling of joy."

It defines "emotions" as a natural instinctive state of mind deriving from one's circumstances, mood, or relationships with others: "She was attempting to control her emotions."

So, we know that emotions are feelings we have in response to things happening around us. They include happiness, sadness, anger, fear, surprise, disgust, and shame.

Now, the new Disney movie *Inside Out 2* has brought the emotion anxiety to the table. It also sends us the message that it is okay to have our feelings, and it is. We must learn to look to the Bible to how we respond to them.

The Bible tells us to acknowledge our feelings, identify them, accept them without letting them become a part of our identity. Pray and surrender them to God. Submit to God our inner turmoil. Grow spiritually, spending time with Him.

It is no secret that we have a mental health crisis on our hands. I brought some statistics to you before starting this section. Here is where the controversy begins: What do we do? Where do we go from here?

We live in an "emoji world" where self-expression and "being the true you" hold highest priority. No one can tell us how to feel. We quickly, even reflexively, send our smiley, sad, crying, surprised, or mad faces via text or comment. And short of rolling on the floor, we deem it better to express any and all emotions rather than hold back and become "fake." No other options exist. Our unfiltered emotional life can, and some say should, extend to any and all persons—spouses, parents, or strangers included. Some even commend yelling at God when we are upset. In all, the assumption stands: you are your emotions—for better or worse. Some say to repress them is to repress yourself. Yet others say, as C.S. Lewis does in his book *The Abolition of Man*, that men such as Plato, Aristotle, and Augustine have reasoned that our emotional responses, rather than being fixed dispositions, could (and must) be trained. That the heart never takes the place of the head: but it can and should obey it.

I will say this. Things are happening in our world that tell us the time is near for Jesus's return. Never has it been more important for us to keep in touch with the Spirit that we received at salvation, the Holy Spirit, and look to His Word to help us to control our emotions.

So, let's take a look at where our emotions come from. Yet again, let's go back to Genesis 1:26-27. Go read that now.

What does it say?

_____

_____

_____

Yes, we are created male and female, in His image, and have dominion over the birds and animals.

Did God have emotions? We could go all through Scripture showing you that God had feelings and emotions—remember Jesus came to the earth fully man, in human form. (Sometimes we forget this truth. I know I do! None of us are perfect or arrived!)

Read Luke 13:10-17.

What emotion is shown in Jesus here?

_____

_____

_____

Read Matthew 21:12-13. What did Jesus express here?

_____

_____

_____

Luke 19:41 and John 11:35:

_____

_____

_____

Now, Luke 10:21 and John 11:15:

_____

_____

_____

Mark 14:33-34:

_____

_____

_____

We could keep going on and on, but you get the point. We are made in His image, and He had feelings and emotions, just as we do!

So, if we are created in His image, we now know that He has feelings and emotions. We have to believe that emotions are a gift from God, a good gift. When God surveyed His creation and called it "good," He didn't mutter under His breath, "except for emotions!" Emotions are a good and gracious gift to every man and woman created in God's image.

To appreciate the gift of emotions, imagine what life would be like if you could not feel. Imagine hanging out with friends yet feeling no pleasure in their company, or saying yes to the man on bended knee but feeling no butterflies. Without emotions you would find no comfort in a good book, a drive in the country or through the mountains in the fall.

Emotions add pleasure, comfort, and richness to events and relationships. Even difficult emotions reflect reality and can move us to a better place. Feelings mirror the pain and suffering in our lives. Imagine losing a close beloved family member or friend and feeling no grief or loss. What if you hurt someone with no remorse or shame? Imagine failing a test and feeling no disappointment. It might sound nice to do without these painful feelings, but none of us can deny that emotions give meaning and depth to our lives. Oftentimes the emotions we could avoid propel us in a new and better direction.

Without emotions, life would be a colorless canvas, boring and bland! God gives us the wonderful gifts of emotions to color life. He is a God of feelings, and those made in His image are not robots. But while feelings are wonderful servants, they are terrible gods! When they flow—ungoverned by God's Spirit and God's Reality— they make us threats both to others and ourselves.

Turn to Psalm 139 (my favorite Psalm), verse 23. What does it say? Have you ever asked the Lord to search your heart? This one powerful verse tells us that God cares about our anxieties, our anxious thoughts. Anxiety robs us of joy. All of us, from teens to retirees, face crippling performance expectations! We face the daily news. If we just take the current year, what devastating news have you faced? What "fear" of the future is hanging onto your thoughts, right this very moment? If we look around to TV, social media, or daily news, it is very easy to get caught up in hopelessness, despair, and depression. By bringing our thoughts and anxieties to the great comforter, He can cool our "overheated" minds.

Practice this prayer: "Lord be near to me. Soothe my heart and mind." He is the ultimate comforter! We are commanded to "look up," not "look around." There is a difference!

Go listen to the song "Indescribable" by Laura Story.

Thank God for the feelings and emotions He gives you to feel the "colors of fall" to the "fragrance of spring." You are an amazing God!

Day 3

Let's look at a verse that shows us where God expresses joy: Zephaniah 3:17 says what?

_____

_____

_____

Yes, that God has so much gladness and joy. That He rejoices over you with gladness! Here that word "rejoice" in the Hebrew includes the meaning of spinning. God doesn't just rejoice over you; He dances in delight over you! That's how much He loves you. He feels joy and compassion when He thinks of you!

From God's Word, I believe we have arrived—that there is nothing wrong with our emotions; however, we don't want to be controlled by them.

Oftentimes we live in the extreme of either/or. I am sad or I am joyful. We excuse the reality that the two can coexist, forcing us to hide a part of ourselves because we feel we should know better. To know ourselves better isn't to say we are making much of ourselves. It recognizes how God designed us, wired us, and created us to think—a.k.a. being human!

I believe a healthy way to begin to deal with our emotions biblically is to start by saying things such as, "I am experiencing feelings of sadness right now." Instead of saying, "I am sad." One recognizes what we are experiencing, while the other labels it as an identity. You can accept what you are experiencing without it becoming a part of your identity! As I had told you earlier, "anger" had become my identity. It resulted in a lot of hard lessons for me, and also became one of my "labels." I remember my crew would always say, "You know how she is." I always just went along with it and said, "Yes, you are right, so stay away from me when I'm mad." I wonder sometimes how I ever had anyone working under me, although I have always been a "good" person at heart!

I want to share the words of a mental health specialist named Raquel Hopkins. She is popular on Instagram and other outlets as the Capacity Expert. She holds a BS in business, as she used to be in corporate business. She has an MBA in international business and a master's in clinical health counseling. She is now a mental health coach and out of the business world. You can look her up and get all her credentials to make the statements she makes on mental health.

Listening to one of her podcasts, she states this: "I thought the goal was to create awareness, to normalize seeking help, to make therapy accessible, to remove the shame around mental health struggles. But somewhere along the way of destigmatizing mental health, it has taken on a life of its own, and now instead of getting better, I just feel like people are getting worse. We didn't just normalize therapy, we've turned it into a personality trait. We didn't just encourage self-awareness, we turned every feeling into a diagnosis and instead of using mental health language as a tool, we started using it as a shield, justifying avoidance, self-sabotaging, and emotional fragility in the name of protection. Now everything is a trigger, everything is trauma. People say, 'I can't do this or I can't do that. It's bad for my mental health.'"

Hopkins says what they really mean is, "This is hard, and I don't want to deal with it." But since when did mental health become about avoiding life instead of learning how to handle it?

She goes on to say that "learning how to handle good mental health isn't about comfort. It's about having capacity. It's about having the emotional, the psychological, and the cognitive range to handle life as it comes. Not just when it's easy but when it's hard. Your mental health should be challenged. Because if your mental health can't withstand stress, discomfort, or uncertainty then you don't have mental strength; you have emotional dependence, based on the right circumstances and life. Life doesn't care about your circumstances. Really ask yourself, has your mental health journey actually made you stronger, or has it made you retreat further into protecting yourself in the name of good mental health?" Wow! Think about this.

My thoughts go right along with her on these statements, and I don't have any of her degrees. Have we made anxiety and mental health struggles an "identity"? Have we made anxiety a "label" that can't be removed? Because that's just how we identify ourselves?

Whew, buckle up! The Bible never tells us we won't have emotions or feelings; it tells us how to control, manage, and care for them.

Let's look at a great example of this. Ephesians 4:26-27 says, "Be angry and do not sin; do not let the sun go down on your anger, and give opportunity to the devil."

This Scripture tells us a few things:

- Anger is an emotion. Paul doesn't say don't have anger.
- Paul is telling us unmanaged anger can lead us to sin.
- Paul gives us a timeline but also a deadline to say, "Don't let your anger go unresolved."
- Harboring anger can give place to the devil.

Think about the last time you went to bed angry at a family member. Your mom, dad, sister, brother, husband, wife, the list could go on and on. I bet you could also think of a time when you heard of an "accident." Where someone left their home and didn't return home. Or went to sleep, had a heart attack, and never woke up. Over and over in my mind I could give you true examples of this. Don't let anger consume you; take it to God today! He cares!

I never knew how to communicate very well. Most of the communication I saw was nonexistent, high-yelling voices, or conversation that led to separation. I believe there is beauty in learning how to communicate well with others and learning how and when our bodies communicate with us. Sadly, many of us try to suppress our feelings. We don't know how to handle them appropriately, so we shove them into a corner of our lives. (Like me!) We have all kinds of reasons we may try to "suppress" our feelings. But I BELIEVE that stifling our emotions is hazardous to our spiritual health. Suppressed feelings don't evaporate; they eventually "burst out" and wreak havoc in our lives. We all likely know the mess a "burst emotional pipe" can make.

The truth is I believe that God gave us emotions as a good gift, to be appreciated and employed in every aspect of our lives. He wants us to glorify Him with our feelings. In fact, we can't honor and obey Him without our feelings! Only when we believe that God has a useful purpose for our emotions, which we will see in the coming days, will we begin to learn how to "handle" them.

Let's look at Philippians 4:12. My pastor just highlighted this verse in sermon. What does it say?

I have 'learned' the secret of being content in any and every situation. I know what it is to be in need, and I know what it is to have plenty. I have learned the secret of being content in any and every situation, whether well fed or hungry, whether living in plenty or in want.

Powerful, Paul had to "learn" how to be content.

Where is God showing you a lesson in being content today? Often, the desire to do something more or better indicates a longing to fill an empty place in a person's life. What do you draw when you feel empty inside? How can you find true contentment?

The answer to these questions lies in your perspective, your priorities, and your source of power. Philippians 4:13. Can we really do all things? We only receive all the power we need through union with Christ. God wants you to step out in "faith" today, trusting Him for the strength you need to deal with your feelings and emotions.

The Lord gave me this verse (Philippians 4:12) as a "life verse" shortly after saving me with His amazing grace.

I look back over my life and know that I had to learn how to be "content;" it didn't just happen. Romans 8:28 takes on new meaning when we look at it with this verse as well. God works all things "for good" and "His glory."

I believe that God works in all things to refine our faith, strengthen endurance, and develop character. God can use even difficult things for His honor and ultimately to conform people to the image of Jesus. It all goes back to that; we are created in His image. However, pain and frustration are still part of the human experience because of what? Yes, sin and our fallen world, because of it!

A favorite quote of mine that I believe goes with being content is: "Bloom where you are planted."

What does this quote speak to your heart today? Should you think about where God has you "planted," right this very second? Should you seek contentment, even in your current circumstances? Take it to God in prayer today!

Day 4

We learned yesterday that we need to "learn" how to be content under all circumstances. Learning this verse will help us keep our emotions and feelings intact. Again, no judgment here; none of us have arrived!

I want us to take a look today at another singer who I have mentioned before in this study, Taylor Swift. As noted, music plays a lot into our feelings and can get us into our feelings and help to change our moods. I want to add here if having money brings contentment, Taylor gained the label of "billionaire" in October 2023, and if we take a look at some of the lyrics of her song in her newly released album, *The Tortured Poets Department* (we will look at some of those lyrics in week 8), we can see that she is still not "content."

One of her most famous songs is "Anti-Hero." It is the first single on her album *Midnights*, released in October 2022.

I took these thoughts off an article I read.[1] She begins the song "Anti-Hero" with: "I have this thing where I get older, but never wiser."

---

1 https://42lifeinbetween.wordpress.com/2022/11/17/taylor-swift-the-theologian/

Could you relate to this? Yes, we likely all could! How many times have you promised to yourself, "I'll never do that again." That was the last … drink, sex before marriage, look at porn, the list is endless. We like to pretend we've changed or evolved. Have you since become a new creation in Christ?

She continues to diagnose the problem: "Midnights become my afternoons, When my depression works for the graveyard shift, All of the people I've ghosted stand there in the room, I should not be left to my own devices. They come with prices and vices, I end up in crises. (Tale as old as time) I wake up screaming from dreaming. One day I'll watch as you're leaving. 'Cause you got tired of my scheming (For the last time)."

Her inability to change or grow works itself out in depression, leading her to remember all the ways she's mistreated others. The fear of being rejected has led her to see others walk out the door, because she cannot stop scheming and just be herself. In fact, it is that scheming to try and hold onto someone that has led them to leave. As she says, it is a tale as old as time. We want people to love us, know us, and yet we can't stop hurting them and ourselves in the process. It is a never-ending carousel of relational sabotage we can't seem to get off of sometimes.

We will get to the course in due time, but the next verse accentuates the problem.

"Sometimes I feel like everybody is a sexy baby. And I'm a monster on the hill. Too big to hang out. Slowly lurching toward your favorite city. Pierced through the heart but never killed. Did you hear my covert narcissism I disguise as altruism like some kind of congressman? (Tale as old as time) I wake up screaming from dreaming. One day I'll watch as you're leaving and life will lose all it's meaning (For the last time)."

In this verse, no matter how thin she is, no matter what she looks like on the outside, she knows it is never "good enough." Even her "good works" are a lie. This echoes Isaiah 64:5-9, when he says, "We have all become like one who is unclean, and all our righteous deeds are like filthy rags." And what drives this? It is her fear of rejection and her desire to be known and loved.

If that isn't bad enough, she goes on: "I have this dream my daughter-in-law kills me for the money. She thinks I left them in the will. The family gathers 'round and reads it. And then someone screams out, 'She's laughing up at us from hell!'"

Her subconscious knows she is not good enough to the extent that it places her in hell! Which leads us to the chorus where she brings it all together and labels the problem correctly.

"It's me. Hi, I'm the problem, it's me (I'm the problem, it's me). At teatime everybody agrees I'll stare directly at the sun, but never in the mirror. It must be exhausting always rooting for the anti-hero."

Here she nails it. She's the problem. In fact, even at her best, she isn't even the hero of her own story; she's an anti-hero. And here is the truth: if we are honest, at the worst she and we are villains in our own story.

In many ways this song echoes the Apostle Paul when he says in Romans 3:23, "For all have sinned and fallen short of the glory of God." Paul in Romans also talks about how we all know that God is there through His creation and how even the law only points to our deficiencies, unable to save us because we can never keep it perfectly.

"Hi, it's me, I'm the problem, it's me."

Taylor is famous for her songs about failed romance. "Anti-Hero" encapsulates her desire to be known and loved when she says, "I'll wake up screaming from dreaming. One day I'll watch as you're leaving and life will lose all its meaning."

What does this line say about her? Relationships are her god. But again, she's the problem.

Look up on YouTube videos on, "If Anti-Hero was a Christian." The lyrics are way better than the song! Beckah Shae and her daughter have one out that is awesome. Look it up today!

Timothy Keller paints the picture well when he says, "To be loved but not known is comforting but superficial. To be known and not loved is our greatest fear. But to be fully known and truly loved is, well, a lot like being loved by God. It is what we need more than anything. It liberates us from pretense, humbles us out of our self-righteousness, and fortifies us far from any difficulty life can throw at us."

What Taylor is looking for cannot be found in a human being. No person can sustain the weight of being everything to another person. No matter the person, they are going to let us down. Heck, she even rightly points out, we let ourselves down, so much that we're not heroes, we're at best anti-heroes.

The Psalmists points this out perfectly when they write, "It is better to take refuge in the LORD than to trust in man. It is better to take refuge in the LORD than to trust in princes. And you were dead in the trespasses and sin in which you once walked, following the course of this world, following the prince of the power of air, the spirit that is now at work in the sons of disobedience—among whom we all once lived in the passions of our flesh, carrying out the desires of the body and the mind and were by nature children of wrath, like the rest of mankind. But God ... being rich in mercy, because of the great love with which He loved us, even while we were in our trespasses, made us alive with Christ—by grace you have been saved—and raised up with him and seated with him in the heavenly places in Christ Jesus. For by grace, you have been saved through faith. And this is not your own doing; it is the gift of God, not as a result of works, so that one may boast. For we are his workmanship, created in Christ Jesus for good works, which God prepared ahead of time that we should walk in them."

Taylor gets part of the answer; she's the problem, we are our own problem. We are dead, but we know this is not the way things are supposed to be. Not only are we dead, but we are enemies of the only one that can fix the problem we know is there. You see we are not meant to be the hero of our own story, but the problem is we all try to be. Genesis helps us by reminding us, "In the beginning, God." We're not the hero of the story because otherwise we will spend our lives toiling away, trying to be what we were never meant to be.

Then Paul gives us the answer, with the best and my favorite words in the Bible, "BUT GOD."

You see, He loved us before we first loved Him, and He sent the one person that could make right what we could not. Not only does He save us, but He promises the very thing Taylor longs for the very most—to never leave us. Jesus promises, "I give eternal life, and they will never perish, and no one will snatch them out of my hand. My Father, who has given them to me, is greater than all, and no one is able to snatch them out of the Father's hand. I and the Father are one" (John 10:28-30).

Ultimate love from one who ultimately knows us better than we could ever know ourselves. Jesus is the hero we need, want, and long for. Jesus knows our villainy, our anti-hero natures, yet He freely offers everlasting love, acceptance, and salvation. Talk about GOOD NEWS!

If "Anti Hero" was Christian, the lyrics tell us that, "It's you Lord, you're the reason I sing, for you Lord, daily worship I bring."

To summarize what you have read over the past few days: We all have feelings and emotions. There's a battle that we must always be fighting against the flesh, and that battle resides in our feelings. Our feelings will lead us to do what "feels" right or good—whether or not it is considered righteous. Our feelings will try to persuade us to do things that are disobedient to God. If we are to live a righteous life they cannot be trusted!

We are called to live by faith, not by our feelings. Our faith is rock solid if we have placed it in Jesus Christ, the unchanging, perfect, eternal, sovereign One. If you don't fill your mind with the Word of God, the enemy will fill it with fear, anxiety, stress, worry, and temptation and could lead us to believe we are out of ourselves and our feelings.

Go read Hebrews 11. It tells us of the countless believers of the Old Testament who lived by faith rather than by feelings. Think about and consider how they may have "felt" versus how they "acted." I am sure they all had feelings of doubt, fear, temptation toward sin, and uncertainty, yet they walked by faith. They allowed their faith to inform and guide them.

After reading, find the song, "Spirit Lead Me" by Influence Music and Michael Ketterer.

It is our responsibility to guard what our hearts and minds are exposed to. The eyes, ears, and mouth are gateways to the heart and mind.

Tomorrow we will look at Scripture that tells us how to guard our hearts and minds.

Following tomorrow's study will be a list of Scripture specific to different mental health challenges that you can use to combat the enemy.

Day 5

Turn to Proverbs 4:23 (NLT): "Guard your _____ above _____ else, for it determines the course _____ _____ _____."

Why do you think this short, powerful verse has so much meaning? Summarize this verse in your own words.

_____

_____

_____

Our hearts—our feelings, our love, our desires—all dictate to a great extent how we live, because we always find time to do what we enjoy. Here Solomon tells us to guard our hearts above all else, making sure we concentrate on the desires that will keep us on the right path. Make sure your affections push you in the right direction. We must put boundaries on our desires: don't go after everything we "see," "hear," or "feel." We must look straight ahead and keep our eyes fixed on what?

Turn to Philippians 3:14 (NLT): "I press on to _____ the _____ of the _____ and _____ the _____ prize for which God, through _____ _____, is _____ us."

We could do a whole Bible study on this one verse, but we will summarize this verse here and move on.

What does it mean to you to "move on toward the prize"?

Could it mean you have to forget the past, let go of some guilt? Could it be you are living in the tension of who you are trying to become? This list could go on and on, but ultimately, we have to get to a place where we grow in the knowledge of God by concentrating on our relationship with Him. Realize that we are a new creation (2 Corinthians 5:17), and move on to a life of faith and obedience to Him. Looking forward to our heavenly prizes and having a fuller, more meaningful life now because of the hope we have in Him.

Look up the video "O Be Careful, Little Eyes" by the Cedarmont Kids. I think people of any age could learn from, and need to remember, this video.

It says to be careful little eyes, what you see.

Whoa! This is a big ole can of worms we are opening up. Let me first explain what a "can of worms" is! I used this expression in our Grow Group (Sunday School) room, and one middle schooler said, "Can you please explain what a 'can of worms' is?" I simply googled it, and this is the meaning behind this slang expression. It is an idiom that means to create a complicated situation that causes many more problems when trying to fix it. For example, and I am sure you could give your own example, but this is one

I have personally used myself in my work environment: "Our boss is reluctant to change the policy now because she doesn't want to open a can of worms."

Casting Crowns released a song in 2007 called "Slow Fade." This song could take on many different angles, but is a cautionary tale against making the wrong choices. The video of this song depicts a family slowly deteriorating due to the compromising decisions they have made. I believe this "slow fade" is what has led us to where we are today in our country. I have watched the "fade" that has occurred even in just the past five years. If we look around the world, you will see that the state of even "the church" in some areas, "black and white" (the truth of The Word), has turned to gray.

The lyrics of this song say, "It's a slow fade," meaning it happens over time, and we create this "can of worms" that gets bigger and bigger and harder and harder to unpack and deal with.

Watch the video today. Pray about what God would have your eyes to "see" throughout the rest of this study. Journal some thoughts below.

_____

_____

_____

I could go to a website and get the "porn addiction" statistics. Each website has different statistics for men, women, and youth. I am going to choose not to list any of those here, because that is a very big "umbrella."

I do want to put here that porn addiction, as we should all agree on, is sweeping our nation heavily. It is called the "new drug," and it can and will cause a lot of emotional heartache. Since the internet, we have it right at our fingertips, and all of us have such easy access to porn. Porn leads to so many other things, like addictions, human trafficking, and lots of other issues. I also could list some medical statistics here. I am going to choose not to, because you will find for yourself, if you google this, many different reports, many different opinions, and they will vary widely depending on which site you choose to use. This is a Bible study, and I am not a medical professional, so I will just say this. Porn addiction, just like any other addiction, is when the brain becomes dependent on pornography to experience dopamine surges; therefore, it will cause a lack of control over sexual behavior. Which means it will, very much so, impact a person's psychological and emotional needs.

Here me out on this. This study is in no way intended to shame you. If you are dealing with a pornography addiction, please seek help today; talk to "someone" today, don't wait. It could be your pastor or a trusted friend. Don't keep it inside or alone with your thoughts; this leads to other issues. The enemy is walking around, seeking whom he may devour (1 Peter 5:8). There is no room for carelessness here. Be self-controlled and alert.

The idea behind pointing out what we look at and listen to is the premise for this part of the study. This is so important because what we see and hear helps us to "guard our hearts and minds."

There are several reasons why it is imperative to guard our hearts. When we get "sidetracked," we will "take detours;" it can lead us into a lot of things that God did not design for us. It can cause us to have major "collisions" in our lives and cause us to lose our way and go into a path of sin and destruction. But, first and foremost, it can have a significant impact on our relationship with

God. When we meditate on the Word of God and allow it to sink into our hearts, we are radically transformed and will experience a greater sense of peace, joy, and contentment.

Go to Psalm 1:2-3: "But they _____ in the law of the _____, meditating on it _____ and _____. They are like _____ _____ planted along the _____, bearing _____ each _____. Their _____ NEVER _____, and they _____ in ALL _____ do."

What wisdom is this? Simple wisdom: The more we delight in God's presence, the more fruitful we will be. This "law of the Lord" refers to all of Scripture. In it, God reveals to us His will, His absolute truths, His love for us, and His divine nature. It means if you want to follow God more closely, you must take the time to know what He says. Mediating on His Word is how we learn to follow God.

Day 5, Continued

*L*et's take a closer look at verse 3.

The phrase "they prosper in all they do" does NOT mean that God's people have immunity from failure or difficulties. Nor does it guarantee health, wealth, or happiness. You may hear the "name it, grab it, and claim it" preachers preach this verse differently. What the Bible means by prosperity is this: When we apply God's wisdom, the fruit (results or byproducts) we bear will be good and will receive God's approval. Just as a tree soaks up water and bears luscious fruit, we are to soak up God's Word and produce actions and attitudes that honor Him. To achieve anything worthwhile, we must have God's Word in our hearts! And it's the only way to have the fruit of the Spirit (Galatians 5:22-23).

On the other hand, allowing sinful influences to take root in our hearts will hinder our relationship with God. We will struggle to pray, read the Bible, and feel distant from God. This is why we must guard our hearts and minds.

The Bible tells us in 2 Corinthians 10:5 to "Take every thought captive to obey Christ." I love how the NLT version says, "We destroy every proud obstacle that keeps people from knowing

God. We capture their rebellious thoughts and teach them to obey Christ." And after you have become FULLY obedient, we will punish everyone who remains disobedient.

So how do we do this? I'm glad you asked! Simply look at the two verses preceding the command to take our thoughts captive.

2 Corinthians 10:3-4 (NLT): "We are human, but we don't wage war as humans do. We use God's mighty weapons, NOT worldly weapons, to knock down the strongholds of human reasoning and to destroy false arguments."

Once again, as in every situation or thought or circumstance we must have our "armor" on to go to war. End of story. There is no other way!

When we guard our hearts, we take responsibility for our mental, psychological, and spiritual well-being. In doing so, we protect ourselves from sinful influences that impede spiritual progress. It will also impact our relationships with others. It can draw us closer or estrange us from them.

Let's go to Hebrews 12:1-4: "Therefore, since _____ are surrounded by such a _____ of _____ to the life of _____, let us strip off every weight that _____ us down, especially the _____ that so easily trips us up. And let us _____ with endurance the race God has set before us. We do this keeping _____ on Jesus, the champion who initiates and _____ our faith. Because of the _____ awaiting him, he _____ the cross, disregarding its shame. Now he is _____ in the place of _____ beside God's throne. Think of _____ the hostility he _____ from sinful people; then

you _____ become _____ and give up. After all, you
have not given _____ in your struggle against sin."

Wow, what do those verses mean to you?

_____

_____

_____

What it should mean to all of us is this. The Christian life involves
focus and training. It requires us to give up whatever hinders or
endangers our relationships with God and to run with stamina
and commitment in the power of the Holy Spirit. We will always
stumble if we look away from Him, to worry about ourselves, or
look at the opposition, trials, or suffering facing us. Run solely for
Christ, and keep Him in sight!

Wrapping up the part of guarding our hearts and minds, we
must first understand that our first identity is His image. And we
must let others see Him in us. By guarding our hearts, we become
who God designed us to be (Ephesians 2:10).

Turn to Philippians 4:7: "Then you will experience God's peace,
which exceeds anything we can understand. His peace will guard
your hearts and minds as you live in Christ Jesus." God's peace is
different from the world's peace. True peace is not found in positive
thinking, in absence of conflict, or in good feelings. It comes from
trusting God to work everything out in a way that is best for you as
you fulfill your role in God's work in the world. In order for us to
do this, we must have the peace of God in our hearts and minds.

What we put in our minds determines what comes out in
our words, desires, and actions. Train your mind to focus on

what thoughts are true, honorable, right, pure, lovely, admirable, excellent, and WORTHY of PRAISE!

Meditate today on what boundaries could look like in your life. You and God are the only ones who know what that looks like for you individually. Put boundaries on what you allow in your mind and heart.

What is God speaking to you through today's lesson? A lot of "hard but necessary truths" here.

Worship to the song, "Build My Life." Ask God to open up your eyes to His Wonder! WE LIVE FOR HIM.

Bible Verses for Mental Health

Matthew 11:28-30

Ephesians 5:18

Philippians 4:13

Romans 8:18

Romans 12:2

1 Peter 3:14

1 Peter 5:7

Isaiah 35:4

Isaiah 40:31

Isaiah 41:10

Philippians 4:6-7

 2 Timothy 1:7

Romans 15:13

Joshua 1:9

1 John 4:8

Romans 8:28

Psalm 34:4

Psalm 94:19

2 Timothy 3:16-17

Romans 8:38-39

1 Peter 5:10

Proverbs 3:5-6

Philippians 1:6

Jeremiah 17:7-8

Psalm 34:17

John 14:27

Hebrews 12:1

2 Thessalonians 3:16

Philippians 4:8

Proverbs 12:25

I feel one of the greatest songs ever that speaks to mental health is "Still Waters (Psalm 23)" by Leanna Crawford. Get in front of a mirror and recite Psalm 23 out loud. Notice the PEACE that will wash over you!

As I was getting ready to put this section into the study, I came across a very good article with exactly my "thoughts" on the anxiety crisis we are facing. I am listing the website here, if you choose to check it out. My thoughts line up exactly with hers, and I don't feel like she is being insensitive at all. I think she is facing what all—well, wait, let me not stereotype here—most mothers are fighting. But God ... and that is how she ends the article.

Her name is Carrie McKean.

Psalm 23

The Lord is my shepherd; I shall not want.

    He makes me lie down in green pastures.

He leads me beside still waters.

    He restores my soul.

He leads me in paths of righteousness

    for his name's sake.

Even though I walk through the valley of the shadow of death,

    I will fear no evil,

for you are with me;

    your rod and your staff,

    they comfort me.

You prepare a table before me

    in the presence of my enemies;

you anoint my head with oil;

    my cup overflows.

Surely goodness and mercy shall follow me

    all the days of my life,

and I shall dwell in the house of the Lord

    forever.

The title of the article is "An Anxious Generation—of Parents."[2]

The summary of the article in the beginning lines up with my thoughts exactly: "Jesus told us not to worry, but worry is our culture's parenting default. It's harming our kids."

If you talked to my daughter, I am certain she would tell you that I have made this exact statement or something similar to her.

Listed below are verses specific to mental health challenges that you can use to combat the enemy. Speak and pray these Scriptures with authority. The enemy knows that he cannot hold in bondage a believer who knows their authority in Christ. These are a few; you may search for more or have favorites. They all work!

Scripture to Combat Fear

2 Timothy 1:7: "For God did not give us a spirit of fear, but of power and of love and a sound mind."

Hmmmm. Wait a minute, didn't we just learn that emotions are from God? Think about how the enemy is using his tactics to come against us!

Deuteronomy 31:8: "He will never leave you or forsake you. Do not be afraid; do not be discouraged."

Isaiah 43:1: "Don't fear, for I have redeemed you; I have called you by name; you are Mine."

My personal favorite, because it has a story about my name that I won't add to this study. You may see it in another one.

---

2 Carrie McKean, "An Anxious Generation—of Parents," *Christianity Today,* August 13, 2024, https://www.christianitytoday.com/2024/08/anxious-generation-of-parents-smartphones-risk-trust-worry/.

Isaiah 41:10: "Fear not, for I am with you; be not dismayed, for I am your God. I will strengthen you, yes, I will help you, I will uphold you with my righteous right hand."

Scripture to Combat Depression

Psalm 34:17: "The righteous cry out, and the Lord hears them; he delivers them from all their troubles."

Psalm 42:11: "Why my soul, are you downcast? Why so disturbed within me? Put your hope in God, for I will yet praise him, my Savior and my God."

2 Corinthians 1:3-4: "Praise be to the God and Father of our Lord Jesus Christ, the Father of compassion and the God of all comfort, who comforts us in all our troubles, so that we can comfort those in any trouble with the comfort we ourselves receive from God."

Psalm 40: 1-3: "I waited patiently for the LORD; he turned to me and heard me cry. He lifted me out of the slimy pit, out of the mud and mire; he set my feet on a rock and gave me a firm place to stand. He put a new song in my mouth, a hymn of praise to our God. Many will see and fear the LORD and put trust in him."

Scripture to Combat Anxiety

Philippians 4:6-7: "Be anxious for nothing, but in everything by prayer and supplication, with thanksgiving, let your requests be known to God, and the peace of God, which surpasses all understanding, will guard your hearts and minds through Christ Jesus."

What would you give up today to TRUST this one verse alone?

Jeremiah 29:11: "For I know the thoughts toward you, says the Lord, thoughts of peace and not of evil, to give you a future and a hope."

Lean not on your own understanding *(Proverbs 3:5-6).* Your own understanding is what "you see." Not the hope of what God KNOWS the future is!

John 14:27: "Peace is what I leave with you; it is my own peace that I give you. I do not give it as the world does. Do not be worried or upset; do not be afraid."

His peace? WOW, what does that look like in your life right now? Could it be you have to let something go to have peace? Pray Psalm 139:23-24 over yourself and pray to see where your "peace" resides.

Scripture to Combat Perfectionism

Galatians 1:10: "Am I trying to win the approval of men, or God? Or am I trying to please men? If I were still trying to please men, I would not be a servant of Christ."

Psalm 18:32: "It is God who arms me with strength and makes my way perfect."

1 John 1:9: "If we confess our sins, he is faithful and just to forgive us our sins and to cleanse us from all unrighteousness."

Scripture to Combat Anger

Proverbs 14:29: "Whoever is slow to anger has great understanding, but he who has a hasty temper exalts folly."

Proverbs 15:18: "A hot-tempered man stirs up strife, but he who is slow to anger quiets contention."

Ecclesiastes 7:9: "Be not quick in your spirit to become angry, for anger lodges in the heart of fools."

Scripture on Joy

Psalm 71:23: "My lips will shout for joy when I sing praise to you—I whom you have delivered."

John 15:11: "I have told you this so that my joy may be in you and that your joy may be complete."

James 1:2: "Consider it pure joy, my brothers and sisters, whenever you face trials of many kinds."

Romans 15:13: "May the God of hope fill you with all joy and peace as you trust in him, so that you may overflow with hope by the power of the Holy Spirit."

Whew, Lord, fill me up! Praise Him for this!

Week 7

We have come to the last two weeks of the study. We have been through a lot of Bible, starting with, "Who God Says He Is!" When God put this study on my heart, I had no idea where to begin. I had a great ending, and believe it or not I started the ending first. (I told you; you might not want to be in my brain!) Imagine that!

I went to lunch with a friend last week and made this statement to her, and she said, "Just like God!" I thought for a moment and then got it! God knows the ending. He sees the last piece of the puzzle; we only see the moments we are in right now or the past. So many ways and confirmations that I have had through writing this study. Week 6 was a tough one—lots of spiritual warfare going on getting that week finished. It took the longest and did not come "natural," as did the other weeks. I hope you found your place in week 6 and God met you right where you are, as I am sure He did!

As noted throughout the study, the lyrics of songs and music can do lots of things for us. This study is an attempt to get you thinking about what goes in will come out. If we put the Word of

God in daily life, love will flow freely from our hearts, and it will be less likely for our minds to become Satan's playground.

Throughout the next two weeks we will be going to God's Word to answer the question, "What Was I Made For?"

Go to YouTube and find Beckah Shae's video with her daughter: "If Billie Eilish's 'What Was I Made For' Were a Christian Song."

This version tells us there is hope. I love it. I really like the ballad that Billie Eilish wrote. The lyrics have us questioning who we are and what we were made for. I must remind you once again that your mental health is determined by what lyrics you take in and what thoughts you don't take captive!

I am going to ask you to do something that I feel like the Lord laid on my heart to put here in the study.

Fast and pray about what the Lord would have you "see" and "hear" for the next two weeks. I believe beyond a shadow of a doubt that He will show you "who you are" and that you were "made for more."

I am also going to ask a BIG one here. NO MIRRORS and NO SOCIAL MEDIA for the next two weeks.

Every day, in many ways, we are faced with "mirrors." The mirror in the bathroom, the mirror of advertising, the mirrors of social media, possibly the mirror of our peers or our siblings, self-condemning thoughts (our internal self-judging thoughts, sometimes brought on by the "mirror of the world"). The world is constantly telling us we are not good enough, that we are never "enough." Never enough is the driving message marketers use to embed dissatisfaction into our hearts and minds. I hope you learned in the past weeks how to guard your heart and mind. Our peers can lunge words at us that stick straight to our hearts. The slang expression of, "Sticks and stones can break my bones, but words will never hurt me." BIG FAT LIE! Words do hurt, and oftentimes words spoken during our childhood can cause us to identify ourselves with them!

Wait, STOP, don't lay that mirror down yet. Before going into the next two weeks of Bible study, do this exercise. Go to your closest mirror. Look at the mirror and see your reflection. Make a list of "what you see." Include both the desirable and undesirable characteristics and feelings you have about yourself. Keep this list handy throughout the next two weeks. (I want you to place it in an envelope, put it somewhere, and not look at it again until the end of the two weeks, so that you can compare the two inventories of yourself!)

I am sure you are not going to "literally" not look in the mirror for the next two weeks, so here is what I mean by that:

The mirror in the bathroom—just look, DON'T critique. (Hard, yes, but you can do this!)

The mirror of those around you—refuse to be a part of negative comments.

The mirror of social media—take a break. (We all need a break from social media.)

Our internal self-judging mirror—only make positive statements or have positive thoughts about yourself.

Again, all of the above "mirrors" reflect how we think about "who we are." Consider it a couple of weeks of "rest" from all the stress of dwelling on these reflections. A vacation! We all need them! Even God rested on the seventh day (Genesis 2:1-3).

Find a quiet place once EACH DAY and ask yourself, "Who does God say I am?" Because no matter what others think or say about you, your identity is something that God gave you individually. Our understanding of identity is enriched and made secure as we plunge deeper into the immeasurable depths of God's goodness, power, and wisdom. The more we know about God, the more secure we will be in who we are. Created in the image of a perfect and Holy God, shaped by His hand, we can rest knowing that our DNA in our bodies and all the days of our lives were written before our hearts ever began beating. Praise Him for that truth today! Praise Him for the truth that the one who wrote the script is sovereign over all!

"You weren't made for tending a grave, you were called by name, born and raised back to life again, you were made for more." Chosen, redeemed, forgiven, loved, adopted, beautiful, special, cared for, empowered, a new creation, His, strong, precious, forgiven, loved, enough … Keep going.

Why are you all of these things? Because you were created in His Image, for His purposes! I love you, but He loves you with an everlasting love that I am not capable of loving you with!

Pray something like this before you begin your study every day:

"Lord, open my eyes to see your love in EVERY story, especially the tough ones. Help me to not become trapped in my own thoughts of myself, my own knowledge, biases, or desire for merit. Keep my heart open to the guidance of your Spirit. And, Lord, as

I continue through the Bible, help me to be transformed by your love. Help me to see through your Word, 'who I am.' Help me to have positive thoughts about myself, and not hear the voices of the world, but your small voice that tells me 'I am a child of God.' Amen."

CHILD

of

GOD

Day 1

Who am I? What's my purpose? What was I made for? Does my life matter? Am I accepted? Am I loved? Am I significant? These are all clear questions that all of us, including adults, ask ourselves. Sometimes these questions "haunt" us. It is very easy to act out on these questions and form our own identity. We are plagued today with a definite identity crisis. How often are we faced with an identity crisis? Well, the truth is our identity changes, our "labels" change frequently. When we change schools, we go from elementary to middle schooler and then to high schooler. When we get a job, our identity goes from "unemployed" to "employed." Or you may gain a job title like nurse, librarian, doctor, etc. When our family changes we may go from "family" to "divorced family," "daughter" to "mother," "son" to "father."

These are called labels, labels that all of us gain as we go through life. Labels are defined as: a small piece of paper, fabric, plastic, or similar material attached to an object and giving information about it.

There you have it; labels give information about us. The truth is, you will receive a lot of different "labels" as you go through life.

They give information about us and shouldn't define us as a person. We can't let the labels life gives us define our purpose and stop us in our tracks. God's labels are better than the world's labels. Seek the labels He gives you over the world's labels.

The list of "labels" that we receive throughout our lifetime has a way of becoming our identity. We have a way of thinking that, because we have the title of "athlete," we are defined by how well we play our sport. What happens when you get an injury and can no longer play that sport? Do you become a "nobody"? The truth is, life brings so many changes—both natural and circumstantial. Many of these life changes bring on feelings of fear and uncertainty. We must come to a place where we realize we are more than the labels we gain as we go through this life on earth and that we are working on our Heavenly labels. The labels God says we are!

I believe the true reason for today's identity crisis is not that we have forgotten who we are but that, as a society, we have rejected the God who created us. Read that again. What a truth that hurts so bad! Cut off from the source of all life and truth, humanity naturally flounders. Hardened hearts sink into confusion and despair as they refuse to grasp hold of the lifeline of truth extended to us—the knowledge of God and the saving blood of Jesus Christ.

You see, when we became "new creations in Christ" our identity changed. When we become a believer in Christ, our identity is made certain because God does not change! No longer is our identity based on what we do or who we think we are, but on "whose we are."

Once we get the truth of God's Word about "whose we are," I believe your world will change, and you will be world changers. As Christians we are all called to share the gospel message. I believe that, until you know "whose you are" and what He says about you, you could be sharing the wrong image of who God really is.

As I was riding through downtown Greenville last night, my hometown, I was looking around at everything—the buildings, the roads, the homes, everything that "changes"—and this verse came to my mind. We must get the truth of Hebrews 13:8. The truth of how HE NEVER CHANGES! This magnificent truth of this one Scripture alone is one we should always remember.

Turn to Hebrews 13:8: "Jesus Christ is the same _____, _____, and _____."

Though human leaders have much to offer us we must keep our eyes on Christ, our ultimate leader. Unlike any human leader we may look to, He will never change. In this ever-changing world we live in, we must get this truth. We can trust this.

Go and listen to "I Believe" by Charity Gayle. He never changes, always faithful.

The first three weeks of this study took you through the "I Am" statements. You went through those and learned the truth of God's Word about who He says He is. Now, let's go see what He says about us.

As believers in Christ, no longer is our identity based on what we do, the label we earn, who we date or marry, our school or job, wealth, what clothes we wear, which Stanley cup we have (by the way, I don't own one). The list could go on and on. Have you read the book of Ecclesiastes? In this book King Solomon recalls all his worldly life has brought and realizes that none of it brought him "happiness," that life without God is meaningless.

This is where we must find ourselves. King Solomon likely wrote this late in life. I believe if you can get these truths while young, God will use you mightily for His Kingdom. We must now find our identity in "whose we are." We now have the label of "child of God."

Living out our new identity in Christ has to take root in our thinking—"our attitude of our minds." We have to put on our new self. It must be based on who God is—His likeness, not ourselves.

We may know in our heads, but how do we live out and not revert to our old ways of thinking?

Let's look at Ephesians 4:20-24. Read that now. What does this say? We are to be made new in the attitude of our minds. We have to abandon our old way of life before we are made new. We must leave our "grave clothes" off and put on our "new wardrobe." This requires a once-for-all-time decision and a daily conscious commitment.

Skip down to verse 30 of Ephesians 4. What does this say?

This tells us that the Holy Spirit, living within us, is a guarantee that we belong to God.

Now go to Ephesians 5:1: "Imitate God, therefore, in every-thing you do, because you are his dear children."

We do this by modeling our lives after Jesus.

No, we are not Jesus, and we cannot live up to what He did for us on the cross of Calvary, but we are made in His image, as we have read several times throughout this study (Genesis 1:26-31 and 2:4-9). We must consider the idea that we were made in His image.

The reality of being made in God's image and then being rescued and ransomed by Jesus should make us want to stand on our heads, jump around, raise our hands in worship, something!

I want this next exercise to become an active part of your quiet time with God for the next two weeks. As you read Scripture, look for who He is—a name, characteristic, or comparison. Then write who you are in contrast to who He is.

First example: Go and read John 4.

In this chapter, one of my all-time favorites, Jesus speaks to the Samaritan woman at the well and speaks of living water. He is the Living Water, you are the thirsty one, the recipient of His refreshing.

Bask in those thoughts as you spend time alone with God today, thanking and praising Him.

Go listen to the song "You Know My Name" by Tasha Cobbs Leonard.

God's Labels Tell a

BETTER STORY

Day 2

Today we are going to study the two "theme verses" of the study, starting with Psalm 139. This Psalm is my all-time favorite, for many reasons, but let's start with verses 13-16 (NLT).

"You made all the delicate, inner _____ of my body and _____ me together in my mother's womb. _____ for making me so _____! Your _____ is _____. How well I know it. You _____ me as I was being formed in utter seclusion, as I was _____ together in the dark of the womb. You saw me before I was born. _____ of my life was recorded in your book. _____ was laid out before a single _____ has passed."

What does this Scripture say about you? Could you run the room knowing He knew your name before your mom and dad did? What did you think about listening to Tasha Cobbs Leonard's song yesterday? The truths of this Scripture blows my mind.

Food for thought today: What do you think David would have thought about how easily the unborn are destroyed today? I mean, as I'm writing this, we are in August 2024. The DNC just took place in Chicago, Illinois, and the party had an abortion trailer, right outside the center, giving free abortions.

In Jonathan Cahn's book, *Return of the Gods,* in chapter twenty-six, "Millions on the Altars," he states, from the time abortion was legalized in the early 1970s, America had spilled the blood of approximately one million children every year. By the second decade of the twenty-first century, it had killed over sixty million of them. He writes, "How can it happen? How could a nation that prides itself in being Christian, under God, and the moral beacon of the world have fallen into such depths of evil?"

Before we go any further, let's go ahead and knock this lie out of the ballpark. If you are reading this, and you have had an abortion in your lifetime, let's go over to Romans 8:1. It says: "There is **NOW NO** condemnation for those who are in Christ Jesus." This means that those who have faith in Jesus as their Lord and Savior are no longer under the judgment of the law.

The verse continues, "Because through Jesus Christ the law of the Spirit who gives life has set you free from the law of sin and death." It continues in verse 2-3 to say this: "God sent his Son in the likeness of sinful flesh to be a sin offering, so that the righteousness of the law might be fulfilled in those who walk after the Spirit, not the flesh."

What does this mean? You are forgiven by the blood of Jesus Christ and set free from death.

If you are reading this and have not ever been saved by God's amazing grace and the free gift of salvation, reach out today. Speak to a pastor at a local church. Get your Bible out and read about salvation. Receive a free gift today! The local church, or a godly friend you know, is waiting for you with open arms today! Do not let the lies of the enemy bring you back!

This takes me back to the Casting Crowns song, "Slow Fade." I think back over my life and remember how much I've personally seen: the falling away of Biblical principles, prayer out of schools, God removed from any public gathering, we could keep going here, but you get the point. It's a slow fade when black and white turn to grey. There you have it; the truth of God's Word has turned to gray. We have churches preaching their own truths of Scripture. The LGBTQ community has hijacked the rainbow, making it their own symbol, distracting Christians into thinking they can't use it. Display your rainbow symbol; you know the true meaning of it!

The LGBTQ community has lured a lot of people into believing that the true meaning of Scripture has been "rewritten." They have created a society that tells us we have to choose who we love. Christianity or them? I believe we can and should love them, but unless we know the truths of Scripture, we can be "lured" into believing what they say is the truth. The Bible speaks of false teachers throughout Scripture. Be careful, little eyes, what you see! Be careful, little ears, what you hear! I believe we can love the LGBTQ community with God's love and share the hope of the gospel. That is our role in this and all other "groups." The mandate of sharing the gospel doesn't change from group to group. The rest is up to the one who created us and them! We often forget that we are only given account for our own sin.

Let's keep going. The second verse I want us to look at today is Ephesians 2:10: "For we are God's _____. He has created us anew in Christ Jesus, so we can do the good things he planned for us long ago."

Say it out loud, "I AM!" Write it: "I AM _____."

I hope that through the next couple of days you get the truth of God's Word about who you are! YOU are His "masterpiece," His work of art, His canvas! NO ONE can take that away from you! NO ONE was created like you. NO ONE has YOUR purpose. NO ONE has your identity. NO ONE has your fingerprint (even if you are an identical twin).

God is our Creator; He intentionally designed every one of us. We see that from just these two verses. You are a masterpiece in His eyes, uniquely created and wonderfully made.

How does knowing God created you uniquely make you feel about yourself? Think about the qualities you may have listed on the prerequisitions to begin this study.

In what ways have you experienced pressure to conform to societal expectations in terms of appearance, talents, or behaviors? How did you handle it?

In closing today, I hope that you have seen through just two small, powerful verses that our purpose is deeply connected to our identity in Christ. That God has a plan for each of us, and it's a part of His grand design. That you are His masterpiece, designed specifically for His purposes!

As we grow in our faith, we discover the good works He has prepared for us: His plan.

Let's remember that our identity is not defined by the world but by the "unchanging" love of our Heavenly Father. Continue to seek Him and grow in your faith as you journey toward a Christ-centered identity!

What are some practical ways you can "declare the praises of Him" in your daily life?

Close in prayer today thanking Him for your talents, personality traits, color of your hair, the one thing that you listed was your least favorite characteristic in the prerequisite section. Thank Him for it all. He made you. He had the plan while you were still in the womb, and He still does! I am overjoyed as I type this, on just how intricately each of us is made!

Praise Him for it today.

Listen to the song "Who You Say I Am" by my favorite singer of this song, Hillsong Worship. You may have another favorite artist. After all, you are a "child of God," made specifically by Him!

"I am who he says I am."

Day 3

Until you know who and whose you are, you're going to have a hard time fully understanding why He created you. You're going to have a hard time understanding your purpose. Your identity and your purpose go hand in hand. Your identity is composed of your gifts, talents, education, passions, upbringing, and so much more. All of these factors serve as supporting roles and tools in your purpose. Knowing your God-given identity helps you better understand how they all fit together and what role they will play in your purpose and assignment.

Ask yourself this question today: What mindset shift do you need to have in order to know and understand your God-given identity?

Let's not go to a website, a friend, a self-identity test, or any way to determine that, except for God's Word.

On the first day of this week, we learned how to look at Scripture and see who God is, and then look at ourselves and see who we are in that.

Today we are going to review A LOT of Scripture to see that!

In this lesson we will read the Scripture, write how God sees you, and then write what that verse means.

Let me do the first one for you:

John 1:12: How does God see you? Yes. A child of God. What does this mean? You are a child of God.

Finish up the worksheet on the next page.

Before doing it, ask God to open your eyes to see what He would have you see. Ask Him to keep your eyes on Him instead of looking around the world as you go through this week. Ask Him to show you that no person or thing can ever change the truth of His Word. Ask Him to help you learn and reflect. Ask Him to help you to truly grasp your identity in Christ, to understand your self-worth, and to embrace the purpose He has created for you. Ask Him as you learn these truths to help shine your light into the world and walk confidently in your Christ-centered identity.

Ask Him to remind you that your identity is not defined by the world but by the unchanging love of our Heavenly Father.

When we have this "under our belt," we will shine bright like diamonds!

Go listen to "Lights Shine Bright" by Toby Mac.

SCRIPTURE	HOW GOD SEES YOU	IT MEANS I'M
Romans 8:16-17		
Genesis 1:27		
Ephesians 1:3-4		

1 Corinthians 3:16		
Romans 15:7		
Colossians 2:10		
Philippians 4:13		
Colossians 3:12		
1 John 4:19		
1 Thessalonians 1:4		
Romans 12:6		
Ephesians 1:3		
Matthew 5:14-16		
1 John 2:12		

Before we go any further, I want us to pause and ask ourselves the following questions:

Do these feel true in your life?

Do you struggle believing or understanding any of these? Why?

Who is our advocate, the one who helps us?

Look at one more verse today, 1 John 2:1. Who does it say Jesus is? Yes, our advocate. What does this mean? It means that we have the best defense attorney in the universe pleading our case! It means that He has already paid the price and penalty for your sins. That is your "defender."

Go listen to "Defender" by Rita Springer. He is for you! Your victory!

Day 4

I want us to continue today with more verses on who God says we are. This is a lot of the Bible. If you need to split this up, you can do half one day and half another day. Remember, God is trying to show you who you are in Him. Don't miss it!

SCRIPTURE	HOW GOD SEES YOU	IT MEANS I'M
Psalm 45:11		
Daniel 12:3		
John 15:14-16		
Jeremiah 31:3		
Ephesians 3:19		

Psalm 68:35		
1 Peter 2:9		
Psalm 121:3		
Ephesians 1:5-7		
2 Corinthians 5:17		
Isaiah 43:1		
Ephesians 2:19		
Romans 3:24		
1 Corinthians 1:2		
1 Corinthians 1:30		
Ephesians 2:6		

Ephesians 2:13		
Ephesians 5:29-30		
Colossians 2:11		
Matthew 5:13-16		
John 15:5		

I could go on and on, because the Bible, over and over, tells us who we are in Christ. When I first began to write this study and read through the Bible, I allowed God to show me so much in the Bible on identity. I really was overwhelmed, and had to take a few days off to process this one truth, that we are made in His image (Genesis 1:26-27). These two verses have taken on new meaning to me over the past six months. You see, we hear this, but do we really believe it? His image, think about that! What image of Him are you showing off?

Do you think the heroes of the Bible ever questioned who they were in Him? What if they had never moved on faith? What if they had not trusted and obeyed? Where might we have been today without Noah? Paul? David? Esther? Rahab? Sarah? Your favorite person from the Bible?

Use these references to refer back to. Maybe you have a favorite verse that tells you who you are in Him that was not listed in the past two days. Write that verse down!

Listen to "Keep Me in the Moment" by Jeremy Camp. Don't miss what He has for you!

*If God doesn't
say it about you,
then stop saying it
about yourself.*

Day 5

As we wrap up this week and move on, I want us to take a look at a few important verses that tell us that, as "God's children," what "benefits" we have from that identity.

Go to Romans 5 and read verses 1-8.

What does this say about us?

_____

_____

_____

These verses introduce a section that contains some difficult concepts. It helps us to keep in mind the two-sided reality of the Christian life. On the one hand, we are complete in Him, declared righteous and accepted fully by Him. On the other hand, we are still growing in Christ, becoming more and more like Him. At one and the same time we have the status of royalty and the duty of slaves. We feel both the presence of Christ and the pressure of sin. We enjoy the peace that comes from being made right with God, but we still face daily problems that help us grow. If we remember these two sides of the Christian life, we will not grow discouraged as we face temptations and problems. Instead, we learn to depend on the power available to us from the Holy Spirit, who lives in us and is God's gift to all who believe.

From these verses we learned we have been rescued and have peace with God. That, as believers, we now stand in a place of undeserved privilege. Not only have you been declared not guilty, but He has also drawn us close to Himself. Instead of being His enemies, we have become His "friends"—children of God. Could you run the room right now?

Turn to John 15:15. What does it say?

_____

_____

_____

Now turn to Galatians 4:5-7. Whew, what does this say?

_____

_____

_____

Let's look at another benefit of being called His children in Romans 5:18-19. What benefit are we receiving here?

_____

_____

_____

Yes, we receive righteousness.

Now read Romans 5:17 and 21. What gift are we receiving here?

_____

_____

_____

Now read Romans 5:11 and 19. What are we receiving here?

_____

_____

_____

Read Romans 5:10-11. What are we receiving here?

_____

_____

_____

Now read Romans 5:20. What do we receive here? Yes, His amazing grace!

As sinners separated from God, we see His law from below, as a ladder to be climbed to get to Him. Perhaps you have repeatedly tried to climb it, only to fall to the ground after advancing one or two rungs. Or perhaps the sheer height of the ladder seems so overwhelming that you have never even started up it. (Once again, if this is you, it is my desire for you to accept Jesus right now. Go back to week 2 of this study to learn how to receive the free gift of sin, or talk to a pastor or trusted Christian leader of the faith today.) In either case, what relief you should feel to see Jesus offering with open arms to lift you into God's presence. You are free to obey—out of love, not necessity, and through God's power, not your own. If you stumble, you will not fall back to the ground; instead, you will be caught and held in Christ's loving arms.

Listen to "You Will Be Found" by Natalie Grant and Cory Asbury, as well as "Just Be Held" by Casting Crowns.

Week 8

I am labeling this week, "The Challenge." I asked you before beginning week 7 and 8 to fast and pray and to give up the mirror, the actual mirror, the mirror of social media, the mirror of our friends' thoughts about us, the mirror of the world. You and God only know the mirror you choose to look at. I hope you are at least trying to do that. We all have dealt with the lies of the enemy at one time or another. It's so easy to become "stuck" in our own thoughts of ourselves and not move on. The truth is, sometimes we are our own worst enemy. Read that again! There are many verses that show us this truth, but my personal favorite is Galatians 5:16-18. Reading those few verses tells us that, if we have the desire to have the fruit of the Holy Spirit (Galatians 5:22-23), then we know that the Holy Spirit is leading us. We are human, and it is human for us to have subjective feelings, but we must learn to be led by the Spirit and not our own selfish desires! The Holy Spirit gives us this power to discern between "our feelings" and "His promptings." We have to have the words of Christ in our minds. If we do this the love of Christ will be behind our actions.

Newly transformed people produce something special with their lives. We have to look at ourselves as a NEW creation, not as someone who may have had an "emotional experience," possibly at an altar of a church, youth camp, ladies retreat, wherever you may have met Jesus. I am not saying here that there is anything wrong with getting "emotional" when you come to know Christ. I am just pointing out that, when that moment occurred, it was the "beginning," not the "end." So often people, especially those who have not gotten the Bible out and read for themselves, believe, "I'm fine" or "I'm good. I had the emotional moment but was never made a new creation." I liken this experience to the butterfly. A butterfly's flight doesn't take place until it's first been through a lot of TRANSFORMATION. And the transformation process is ugly. Then a beautiful creature comes out flying. Some have asked me when I say this, do I believe that I will come back as a butterfly? Really?

The truth is, "I am my Father's child. I make Him proud. And I make Him smile. I was made in the image of a perfect King. He looks at me and wouldn't change a thing. The truth is, I am truly loved by a God who's good when I'm not good enough. I don't belong to the lies; I belong to You, and that's the TRUTH. I know who I am. 'Cause I know who You are. And I hold your truth inside of my heart. I know the lies are always gonna try and find me. But I've never been so sure."

These are powerful lyrics of a song by Megan Woods called, "The Truth."

Let's have a dance party! You ready? Read Psalm 149: 3-6. What does it say? Yes, sing and praise His name with dancing. As with anything, a dance NOT honoring the Lord is sin. But a celebration praising and honoring who you are in Him, I believe is just fine! David dancing before the Lord in 2 Samuel was seen as an example of surrendering to God in worship.

First, make some time when you are in the house alone. (Don't let anyone at home make you feel "some kind of way" about this!) Go put on an outfit you "feel" best in. Maybe a nice dress, pink shoes ARE A MUST! Listen to this song now, stand in front of a floor-length mirror. If you don't have one, get the biggest mirror you have! Boldy declare this truth, "I am a child of God. And I believe I have all the benefits of being that!" Boast that you are, "His favorite." I know I am! The lyrics of this song have been my prayer for you throughout this whole study. That you see the truth of God's Word about "who you are" and "who He is." Also, I hope if you have reached this point of the study that God has revealed some of the truths of His Word about "who you are" in the eyes of the Father. Have fun, do it more than once, show the devil he is a liar, and you are on the winning, saving team of the One True King!

Remember the "inventory" we took of ourselves over in week 7 and slid in an envelope? The one where we looked in the mirror and listed our "good" and "bad" characteristics? I hope you did that exercise; now go find that, and after having your mirror dance party with Megan Woods, do a second "inventory" of yourself, and compare the two. During this second one you should have already finished week 7 and allowed God to show you the truth about "who you are," and you should NOT list ANY negative thoughts, although the enemy will try to hit you with them. Remind him first "whose you are" and then "who you are!"

Okay, put the mirror away. you've had your dance party. You have just one more week of study before you should pull that back out!

Another amazing song is Ben Fuller's "Who I Am." Can you tell I listen to music?

In this song, one of the lyrics says this: "Who I was I left at the altar." We have to leave who we were at the altar, or wherever that may have been, and take on our new identity! Now go look up Ben Fuller's song!

All my love and prayers for this week. Buckle up, it may be a long week, but you've got this!

Love, Ann

Day 1

*U*p until this week of the study, I have laid out five days of study time. I am, however, going to do this week differently. I gotta mix it up a little. I can't let you get too comfortable. Life happens, change occurs, daily sometimes; actually change can occur in an instant. Our life is a vapor (James 4:14). This side of the study may look more like a book. I pray, however you decide to read it, you get the truth of God's Word on each heavy topic! For that reason, I am labeling them daily, but you may take more or less time to read each one. Don't rush it. I believe God wants to bless you through this section! Happy reading!

This week I am going to challenge you to understand biblically four things that I feel all of us deal with, and at some point in our lives we have to put to rest and set boundaries for ourselves and others on how we deal with these emotions. We have learned over week 6 some heavy truths of Scripture on our emotions. I am going to put this waiver here: once again, I am not a medical professional, and I am just listing the truths of Scripture.

The four things that I feel could trip us up, and possibly cause us to not "get" our identity in Christ, or not take advantage of our full identity, are jealousy, fear, people pleasing, and comparison. These are four things that I believe social media has worsened for ALL of us.

I believe if we continuously look at others' "stuff" it will be so easy to listen to the enemy's lies about ourselves. I don't believe we were created to know others' "stuff" and also believe that Facebook becomes Fakebook. Most of us only put our "good" stuff on social media, and we all know our home lives are not always peaches and cream. Also, it is so easy for us to compare ourselves to others' lives. I know I've caught myself doing it, and I choose to spend my time more wisely. Just this year, I gave up social media for Lent. I let the Lord show me through Scripture that I could write and let Him have His "way" in my heart on some personal matters. Have I arrived? No, I am still being "transformed" into the lady He made and called Mary Ann back in 1966. Whew, that sounds so long ago.

The first one I want us to take a look at is jealousy and envy. Here is the emotion that I hate most, and have been affected by the most, in my lifetime. Another book for another time, but this emotion I have seen my ENTIRE life. Whether you've been the target of someone's envious or jealous feelings or you've been the jealous person yourself, God understands.

So let me also state upfront that this is in no way intended to be judgmental but instead to point you to God's Word on this topic. To be human means that you will more than likely experience all the negative emotions this world has to offer. No Christian but Jesus Himself has walked this Earth without blemish.

Jealousy … you know it lurks beneath the surface occasionally rearing its head with a snide remark. Then it retreats with the words, "Oh, I'm just playing."

At other times, it's that disappointing and resentful feeling welling up inside. It usually happens when you see someone getting something (seemingly) so easily when you have given your best and it still wasn't good enough. You know the time you see your "friend," who you've poured out your heart to the day before, get invited to the party with other friends of yours, and you are sitting home looking at the pictures on social media, uninvited. Or maybe that car your friend just bought and posted on social media, and you are working two jobs to afford to feed your family and drive a used car.

You know, I don't have to keep going; it's the feeling of fighting back tears for the offender and the sting of betrayal for the afflicted.

I want us to explore the definition of jealousy and envy from a biblical perspective. (By the way, perspective was my word for 2024. Boy, did the Lord show me some stuff this year on that word.)

We will look at some examples of jealousy and envy in the Bible and discuss some ways you can overcome envy and jealousy and live a life of contentment, as Paul says we could and should do (Philippians 4:11-13). We have to "learn" to be content in where we are, and not be envious or jealous, because guess what this leads to? Another negative comparison. These are all heavy topics I know, but they are much needed for us to explore.

I could have hit these negative emotions over in week 6, but feeling like a challenge in week 8 was what I was led to write about.

In order to fight a negative emotion, we must first understand it. When we look at the words envy and jealousy, we may try to use them interchangeably. They are not!

These emotions have existed since the beginning of time, and the biblical meaning of envy and jealousy are just as we define them today.

According to dictionary.com the definition of "envy" is as follows: "Envy is a negative feeling of desire centered on someone who has something that you do not."

"Jealousy" is defined as: "A feeling of resentment, bitterness, or hostility toward someone who has something you don't."

I know that sounds like the same thing. But in order to fully understand these emotions, which doctors study, we are going to God's Word for our understanding.

The Bible is full of flawed people, just like us. People who God used for His glory and as an example to me and you.

The greatest example of envy in the Bible is Satan's envy of God. Known as the father of lies, Satan was the first sinner. It all started when he became envious of God, leading to his rebellion. We know from Ezekiel 28 that Satan once held a high position in heaven. He was one of God's masterpieces (just like us)—a work of beauty. However, he didn't want to serve God: he wanted to be God. And like the serpent that he is, when Adam and Eve fell, this emotion seeped into the Earth.

Another great example is Sarah's envy of Hagar (Genesis 16:1-16 and Genesis 21:8-21). In this example, I believe you see a bit of both envy and jealousy.

In Genesis 37 we see the animosity of the sons of Israel.

Now, let's look at some examples of jealousy.

Cain's jealousy of Abel can be found in Genesis 4. Saul's jealousy of David can be found in 1 and 2 Samuel.

You could read the story of Rachel and Leah, two sisters married to the same man. Talk about a biblical soap opera. Can you imagine?!

You could read story after story, but you get the point. Jealousy and envy are emotions you DO NOT want to become entrapped in. They can cause comparison, shame, insecurity, and a lot of mental stress.

Let's look at a biblical approach to overcome jealousy and envy.

If you deal with jealousy and envy, the answer that I can only give you is Jesus.

I have learned through my Christian walk that it is foolish to think I can change myself. If I could, or you could, what would be your need for Jesus? I just told you earlier today how old I am, and believe it or not, I have NOT always known this truth. The truth that I could not do EVERYTHING for myself was a reality I just came to face back in 2010. Again, another story for another time! Let's move on!

Here are some practical ways you can overcome these feelings, as well as other feelings. First, let's start with prayer.

Pray. Prayer is our most powerful weapon, and you will see it as a solution over and over again! Be honest, God knows. Tell Him your feelings. (Let me let you in on a little secret, shhhh, He already knows.) In the words of the country song "Jesus, I'm Jealous," by Mackenzie Carpenter, she is very gut honest about a couple she is watching that she doesn't even know. This is where we can find ourselves. Ask Him to help you overcome these feelings. He is a God of mercy and grace, not shame and guilt. That was taken away on the cross of Calvary!

Develop a heart of gratitude. Envy is focused on what we don't have. Instead focus on what you do have. Start thanking

God for what you have. Start a gratitude journal. I started mine after reading the book *1,000 Gifts* by Ann Voskamp. You will see through this journaling that the Lord has blessed you with way more "things" than just that car that you didn't get. You will see that some of the best of God's creations are "free" and not "material things" at all. The greatest examples of this are the sunrise, sunset, beach, mountains … I could go on and on. Start your own! Take a look at the one I designed to go with this study. Buy it, and write one thing every morning in it. Or do an inventory daily. Use it however you see fit, just develop a heart of gratitude! This causes you not to look around but to look up to the one who made you and be grateful!

"Gratitude" by Brandon Lake, as listed as one of the worship songs you should listen to earlier in the study, is also a great place to start. Listen to this song and worship Jesus for the many blessings He has bestowed on your life. Never have I felt more gratitude for what I have in this very moment as when Hurricane Helene ripped through on October 3, 2024. As I sit and write this, I almost feel "guilty" as I sit in a home that wasn't damaged, with a refrigerator partially full of food (haven't been to the grocery store this week). My car is sitting in the garage, and I have a closet full of clothes. While, just a hundred miles away, people are struggling just to live another day, with everything they have worked for all their lives destroyed. Homes, cars, businesses, and most importantly, people's lives are gone. Gone without warning, gone in a moment of time. Life is a vapor. The old saying, "You don't know what you got till it's gone," sure does take on a new perspective (there's that word again, I was reminded during this time). Inventory time!

Trust what God has for you is yours. What God gives, no man can take away. Trust His plans; His plans were made specifically for you. No one else can do them. He designed you for His plans and purposes. You are His masterpiece (Ephesians 2:10)! His plan for YOU is better than anything you could hope for or imagine. And better than the plan you keep letting the enemy bring you down with: stalking on social media to see if they have a new haircut, lost weight, or have a new boyfriend. Trust in the Lord with all your heart (Proverbs 3:5-6).

Spend Time with God. When you are surrounded by Him, it strengthens your foundation, your faith. Faith allows you to keep going, keep pressing. Expecting God to do whatever He put in your heart or something even greater! Dream big! After this study, set times when you break from social media, or any type of distraction. It may not be social media for you. It could be something else you have to take out of your schedule. But make EVERY effort to do so. Do this as if your life depends on it … because it does! BUT GOD …

Understand and find comfort in your season with God. We can often find ourselves in a jealous spirit of someone else's "season." Here is where we can have some very unrighteous jealousy. Just because someone else is in their harvest season while you're in the spiritual season of winter doesn't mean that God has forgotten you. He's preparing you. Boy, I am waiting to see the harvest that is to come of my spiritual winter this year. If you arrive at the harvest too early, you won't be able to sustain it, and God knows this!

Just like physical seasons, each spiritual season is dependent on the other. You cannot have a fall harvest without a winter and spring. Once you understand your season with God, you can thrive in every one of them.

Emotions will come, but that doesn't mean we have to keep company with them! It also doesn't mean we let them destroy our relationships, peace, and joy!

When envy or jealousy come for you (and they will), use the tools above to stop them in their tracks, no matter what side of the coin you're on—the envious or the envied.

Pray this prayer against jealousy and envy:

"Dear Father, I confess that envy and/or jealousy have entered my heart. I know that these are not emotions that you wish to see in your child. So here I am asking for your help. I ask you to help me overcome these emotions. I ask you to help me trust that you are good and that you are working all things out for my good. I thank you for your protection and provision. I thank you for my portion. I cast out anything in me that is not like you. I invite you to be the Lord of my heart. In Jesus name. Amen."

Day 2

Today we are going to take a deeper look into what jealousy does to us and some of the consequences of jealousy. Being jealous indicates that we are not satisfied with what God has given us.

Jealousy is a weapon, which the devil has used and is still using to destroy lives. Many relationships, homes, marriages, employment, opportunities, etc. have been terminated prematurely because of this demonic seed. Allowing jealousy to dominate or rule your life will result in terrible damage.

Some consequences of jealousy are that it brings hopelessness and depression.

Read Proverbs 23:17-18. What does this say?

_____

_____

_____

Jealousy makes you cruel. Now read Song of Solomon 8:6. What does it say?

_____

_____

_____

Did you hear that?

Now read Proverbs 27:4. What does this Scripture tell us? The meaning of this Scripture is that, with jealousy in your life, you're in the worst possible situation you can be in.

Jealousy causes you to have limited power. The limited power comes as a result of the fact that you'll find yourself always comparing, because jealousy causes a person to live a life of comparison. The attitude of comparing yourself with another person is a lack of wisdom.

Read 2 Corinthians 10:12. What does this tell us?

_____

_____

_____

Beloved, jealousy breeds comparison, and every time you compare, you belittle what God has done and is doing in your life. An attitude of comparison is a sign that you're not grateful. Jealousy projects the image of selfishness. Learn to be happy and content with what God has blessed you with, who you are, what you're doing, and where God has you at this very moment.

Jealousy in your life is a sign of carnality. Go read 1 Corinthians 3:3. What does this verse say?

_____

_____

_____

The expression "baby Christians" here designates "carnal Christians," and carnality means living a flesh or sense-dominated life. I mean, any way of thinking that opposes God's plan and purpose for our lives is carnal thinking, right?

Let me let you in on a secret, a hard truth from reading these verses. The right way to think is to be happy when somebody else gets blessed. Rejoice when people succeed. Appreciate people for what they have which you don't have; for what they are, which you're not. Such an attitude is likened to sowing a seed which gets you prepared for others to come and rejoice and celebrate with you also when your own turn comes, given that we ALL have "our turns." A life controlled by jealousy will stop you from that expectation. If you allow the devil to bring you down from your exalted position, where you're seated with Christ (Ephesians 2:6), far above any other king or ruler or dictator or leader; to operate in jealousy means you're doing what ordinary men do. Ordinary men and women are of this world, whose lives are based on the standards of the world. You are different because Jesus lives in YOU! You are supernatural (Romans 12:1-2)!

Jealousy brings bitterness. Read James 3:14-15. What does this say?

_____

_____

_____

You can't move around with bitterness in you without hurting your health. Bitterness is a slow suicide. And if we look to some medical reports, which you could, you will find that it could result in cancer, stress, mental health issues, suicide, and premature death.

Jealousy brings confusion. Read James 3:16. What does this verse say?

_____

_____

_____

All sorts of evil and bad practices come from jealousy. It's the root of murder, confusion, disorder, and uncertainty. It most of the time is the foundation of every evil thing.

It is so easy for us to be drawn into wrong desires by the pressures of society and sometimes even listening to well-meaning Christians. By listening to advice such as, "assert yourself," "go for it," or "set high goals," we can be drawn into greed and destructive competitiveness that push us beyond the good intentions of the advice. Seeking God's wisdom delivers us from the need to compare ourselves to others and to want what they have.

Comparison is another big trap of the enemy. We will go more into that trap tomorrow. Today I challenge you to listen to "I Am Loved" by Mack Brock. Embrace the love the Father has for you today. There's nothing to hide, nothing to measure, because you are "His child." NO distance in His embrace.

JEALOUSY

is the art of counting others' blessings instead of your own.

Day 3

*Y*esterday's lesson led us to know that jealousy and envy also lead to comparison.

We all know the trap: My style isn't like hers… I wish my hair was like hers…. I wish my body was made more like hers…. I wish I had her clothes… Oh look, she has a new iPhone, and I have none…. We could go on and on here, but you get the point, I know you do!

Let's define "comparison": A consideration or estimate of the similarities or dissimilarities between two things or people.

There you have it. You see, comparison doesn't always start off badly. Wanting to be better and do better is an amazing thing. The problem begins when seeing what others have causes you to look away from what you have. Read that again. We All have our own identities to maintain, our own paths to take, and our own lives to live, but the zeal to be like others often pulls us away from the beauty that lies in that fact.

Let's look at 2 Corinthians 10:12: "Oh, don't worry; we wouldn't dare say we are as wonderful as these other men who tell you how important they are! But they are only comparing themselves with each other, using themselves as the standard of measurement. How ignorant!"

Whew, if that doesn't hit you between the eyes. In this example of comparison, Paul criticized the false teachers trying to prove their goodness by comparing themselves with others rather than by God's standards. When we compare ourselves with others, we may feel proud because we think we're better than them. But when we measure against God's standards, we quickly realize that we have no basis for pride.

Some other examples of comparison in the Bible include the twelve spies in Numbers 13. They were sent out to scope the land God promised them, but only two chose to believe God over their own opinion. The other ten chose to compare themselves to the people who lived in the land at the time. Read that story. Because of their wrong thinking and comparison, those ten spies and all the people who believed them never got the opportunity to enter the land.

In 1 Samuel 18, the first King of Israel, Saul, chosen by God, was a good man until he started comparing himself to David. Saul heard people saying that he had defeated a thousand while David had defeated ten thousand. This made him very jealous; he allowed the opinions of others to get into his head and began to compare himself. The comparison then led to bad behavior as Saul began thinking he needed to kill David in order to be the best again. He never managed to kill him, but he did waste a lot of time trying. Comparison is a thief of a lot of things! Time, mental health, possibly broken relationships, etc.

We could go to Genesis 37 and find the example of Joseph comparing himself to his brothers. Or Judges 6, where Gideon compared himself to everyone else and called himself the "least of the least." But God called him a mighty warrior.

Is it possible you don't see the mighty warrior in yourself because you are comparing yourself to someone else? Is it possible you are missing God-given opportunities because you are comparing yourself to others around you? Once again, we find from examples of the Bible that we can all deal with jealousy and comparison.

I want us to take an example more to our modern day. I want us to take a look at Taylor Swift's latest released album. Again, I am not judging nor am I "picking" on her. I am just stating facts from the lyrics of songs she has made millions from. And she is one person of great influence today. Imagine with her scale of influence what could happen through her if she professed and pioneered for Jesus? As mentioned earlier in the study, Taylor has LOTS of "followers," called "Swifties," and she is using her music as a platform to have influence on a lot of girls and women, and even men now! What could you do today to have an influence on bringing someone to Jesus? Think about that. Don't compare yourself to Taylor; you have your own "works" cut out for you, designed just for you (Jeremiah 29:11).

In Taylor's latest album, *The Tortured Poets Department*, she, who lives in the same social media-saturated universe as the rest of us, has lyrics in her songs that indicate she may be feeling the same effects of media that I feel social media has done to us all.

I think you could pull any psychology report from anyone, and it would tell you the same thing. You don't have to be a psychologist to tell that this is definitely what Facebook and other platforms have done to the normal person, me and you!

Social media is a breeding ground for comparison, creating a portrayal that we must give the best version of ourselves. Often our posts are fake or skewed. None of our "real stuff" is put on any social media platform. We even make sure we have our makeup just right! We must do that in fear someone will judge us for our lives.

Taylor may be the most famous and successful pop star on the planet, but comparing yourself with even more heroic figures is sure to make anyone "feel" worse.

"You're not Dylan Thomas, I'm not Patti Smith. This ain't the Chelsea Hotel, we're modern idiots." Here Swift reprimands a partner with literary pretensions, and herself for dating him. Taylor, don't call yourself an "idiot." God made you for more!

Comparisons will make you miserable. The average teenager, and I believe women are no different, spends nearly five hours every day scrolling Tik Tok, Instagram, Snapchat, and others. Comparing ourselves to others for that long every day, I believe—again I am not a medical professional (and I don't think you need to be a professional to know this, and I have not done any research to suggest this)—could lead to anxiety and depression.

It can also cause feelings of loneliness. There are many reports out there to support the medical mental effects. I choose not to use them; some I agree with, some I don't.

The pandemic showed us that social media relationships can't replace physical company. Even celebrities with hundreds of millions of followers simply want someone to be with. In the song "The Prophecy," also on *The Tortured Poets Department*, Swift sings of loneliness and wanting someone who simply enjoys her presence: "Don't want money. Just someone who wants my company."

I think lyrics like these are what cause girls to be so relatable to Taylor. When we are listening to these songs, we are getting affirmation, from one of today's big influencers, that it's okay to have "all the feels and emotions." I believe she is bringing the right message: Yes, we do all have mental health challenges. The problem? She isn't telling us that, through the blood of Jesus Christ, you are an "overcomer." (Now, go run through your room and yell, I am an overcomer!) I also believe that the "dark lyrics" of her songs, and some other artists like Billie Eilish, could lead us to depression and loneliness and get us into our emotions.

Swift and Eilish both have openly discussed mental health in different outlets. Taylor has discussed her struggles with anxiety and body image, sharing these personal aspects to connect more deeply with her fans. She feels that she is breaking down the stigma surrounding mental health. Mental health is sweeping our nation with leaps and bounds, and I am not discounting that mental health should not be taken seriously. I am posing the question, "Should you take a biblical approach to it?" And I believe the answer is yes. I have not done any research on what the Bible does to and for your mental health, but I (ME, PERSONALLY) believe that it has to do something for it. If we are putting "good" stuff in, "good" stuff comes out!

I am not judging Taylor, but, according to the lyrics of her songs, she is not looking to the Bible for any of the "feelings" that she deals with. Again, having "feelings" and "emotions" are indeed "human." I "feel" we have to turn to the right place, the Bible, to deal with these natural emotions.

Comparison is the single greatest trick of the enemy. And most people, including adults, myself included, have let it work! This is the biggest trick of the enemy that ALL of us have fallen for at one time or another.

Theodore Roosevelt said, "Comparison is the thief of joy."

I believe this is one of the greatest, truthful quotes of all time. We have an enemy walking around, seeking whom he can devour (1 Peter 5:8). Anything the enemy can get us to do to take our eyes off of Jesus and His image and onto ourselves and others, he will definitely use it.

Let's define "joy": a feeling of great pleasure and happiness.

The Bible defines joy as a fruit of the Spirit, an emotion that comes from trusting God, and it's a natural part of the Christian faith.

Turn to John 15:11: " I have _____ YOU _____ so that my _____ may be in YOU and that _____ JOY may be _____."

Channel some thoughts here on that verse.

_____

_____

_____

In these verses the author challenges us to treasure our unique gifts and talents as individuals. He reminds us that we each have something special to offer the world and that it is OUR responsibility to cultivate these unique strengths and use them to glorify God.

We must take these gifts and talents and use our God-given ability to work hard to cultivate them and allow them to shape who we are as people. Only by cultivating what makes us special can we truly live up to the potential that God has given us, and only then can we experience the fullness of His love and grace.

Let us lift our hearts and minds in praise of God's many blessings, knowing that no matter what challenges we may face in life, He will always be there with a word of encouragement and hope. After all, verse 11 says that God's grace is an individual gift unique to each of us. And it is this grace that will sustain us through anything! Amen!

We have to STOP comparing ourselves to others. Break free from the habit today! It is a challenging but rewarding process. There is freedom like no other in breaking the chains of comparison.

Let's look at another favorite of mine on comparison. Turn to Galatians 6:4:

"Pay _____ _____ to YOUR _____ _____, for then YOU will get the _____ of a job _____ _____ , and YOU _____ _____ to _____ YOURSELF to _____ else."

One of the greatest ways to do this is focus on who God is and who He created YOU to be!

Stop comparing yourself to others and start focusing on your value and worth. Focus on what God has given you and how blessed you are. Focus on YOUR identity!

When you are tempted to compare yourself to others, look at Jesus Christ. His example should inspire us all to do our best. Let His loving acceptance of us comfort us when we do fall short of our own expectations. Because ultimately, if we take a look at verse 5 of Galatians, what does it say?

_____

_____

_____

Let's look at 1 Corinthians 10:13. What does it say? Yes, that we are all tempted! Find ways that you can resist the temptation of comparison. Recognizing who we are in Christ keeps us from comparing!

Second, detox from social media. I hope that these last two weeks you have taken a social media break. We all need them. Scrolling social media is a trigger for the comparison game for many of us. In addition to less time on social media, it means you can spend more time focusing on who God is calling you to be. And any time spent with God is a win-win, right?

Third is to practice gratitude in order to avoid Satan's trap and be sucked into it. To avoid this trap, we must turn inward and focus on what God has given us and not what we "feel" like we lack! Hebrews 13:5 tells us to be content with what we have, for He will never leave us or forsake us. The world will always tell us to turn inward and focus on ourselves and what we lack. Gratitude, on the other hand, causes us to look outward toward what we have been given already! Start your gratitude journal today. It will keep you from looking at what you "lack" and give you a sense of thankfulness for what you do have!

Pray prayers of thanksgiving and gratitude. Write one below.

_____

_____

_____

Don't let YOUR ice cream melt while you are counting SOMEBODY ELSE'S sprinkles.

Day 4

Here is something I believe we could all also get caught up in doing. I personally have never been a people pleaser, as I ran a business for thirty-nine years and have learned during that time that you will not please everyone. And we are not expected to. We are called to "serve" the Lord, and we are also called to serve people. However, I believe we can get caught up trying to "please people" while "serving the Lord" and His people.

Let's define people pleasing. A people pleaser is someone who has a strong desire to please others (not a bad thing, if we are assertive enough to know when to say no).

Oftentimes a people pleaser will have such a strong desire to please others even at the expense of their own needs. People pleasers are often seen as kind and helpful, but they may have difficulty saying no or advocating for themselves. This can lead to resentment and burnout in relationships. It can also cause our mental health to suffer and give us anxiety or depression.

A people pleaser personality is not a medical diagnosis or a personality trait that psychologists measure; instead it is a label that one could easily achieve if boundaries are not clearly set in relationships, whether personal or work relationships and even friendships. You could be a people pleaser in any relationship! Set boundaries in all relationships for your own mental health.

As Christians, we want to serve others, because when we are doing this, we believe we are serving God. We know our "works" don't save us, but we are overflowing with love and gratitude toward God. And serving others is a way to express that. It is also a way to help others get a tiny glimpse of the love God has for them. However, our sinful nature can twist this into something that is not actually serving God but serving ourselves.

Let me give you an example. I don't want to sound arrogant or boastful here, so hear my heart when I say this: God has given me many talents, talents I am so thankful He has entrusted me with. Shortly after I was saved and started serving the Lord, the women's leader came and told me we were going to have a women's conference, and she asked if I would help plan, speak, and set it up. My mind immediately went to just let me do it ALL, I don't need help. Remember, I am that independent, strong, woman leader who doesn't need or want help. At that very moment the Lord convicted me and said, "You can DO ALL those things, but at this particular season of your life, this is what I have for you. You are the speaker, start preparing your speaking part."

Now this actually devasted me because I wanted to make the pretty little centerpieces for the tables and decorate the room and speak and be in charge. I wanted everything to be perfect. I didn't want to delegate anything to anyone. I had the skills to do all kinds of stuff, so why not? I was competent and talented. And asking for help, well that really didn't fit my "vibe."

Don't get so caught up in pleasing yourself and others that you forget the more important calling that God has on your life in that season of life! This was my first lesson in church, and let me tell you, it didn't come easy.

Let's look at Galatians 1:10: "For am I now seeking the approval of man or of God? Or am I trying to please man? If I were trying to please man, I would not be a servant of Christ." Boom. There it is! When we understand our own motives, we can determine whether we are truly serving God or whether we are serving ourselves. People pleasing seems to serve others, but the underlying motives are self-serving.

I didn't know many of the people of the church, and had not been in church very long at all, so I didn't have that "church reputation." I just knew I could plan, decorate, set all the games and activities, make cupcakes, and speak. Sound tiring? It is, and eventually you will "burn out."

The Bible says this in Romans 12:4: "For as in one body we have many members, and the members do not all have the same function."

God equips us with different talents, and these gifts get used in different ways at different times. We do not have to say yes to everything, because when we do, we do not have the time or energy to say yes to things that God may be trying to use us for in that season.

In this situation and time in my life, I needed others to see my worth and what I was capable of "doing." Going back to the comparison section, I definitely was comparing myself to what I felt like I had to "live up to" for people to see how talented I really was, and also so I didn't have to "deal" with others, as I didn't need help.

You may find yourself in this situation one day where you feel like you have to "people please" or serve your own selfish desires. If and when you come to that crossroads, (it will sting, I'm just telling you ahead of time), turn to Matthew 10:29-31.

Read that one more time. It's hard to believe God finds worth in us. But we are valuable to Him. Reminding ourselves of our identity in Him can remind us that we do not have to strive to make others see our value. It is important to center our "worth" right in the middle of God's love for us.

God does call us to go the extra mile and serve others, but we must do it with pure motives and not get in the way of what God's will for our lives may be at that time. Ask yourself these two questions, and go to God in prayer with them.

1. Is how I am serving the Lord, right now, in His will for me right now, during this season of my life?
2. Am I trying to please God or others?

I love you, but Jesus loves you more!

Ask yourself this question:

"For am I now seeking the favor of men, or of God? Or am I striving to please men?"
Galatians 1:10

If God has called you to it,
Fully Commit.

Day 5

*F*ear—this is a great BIG ONE here. I could probably write a whole book on this. Maybe one day I will, but for now, this finishes up my first one! (Don't get too ready; we're not quite at the end yet!) I hope you have enjoyed this study, and I pray God has shown your worth and identity in Him. After all, He is worthy of all honor and praise!

Fear is an unpleasant emotion caused by the belief that someone or something is dangerous, likely to cause pain, or a threat. It's the feeling or condition of being afraid.

We all deal with it. What's your biggest fear? Think about it. We touched on emotions back over in week 6, and I didn't go into a lot of detail on this emotion, because I wanted to do a whole section here. So here it goes. I believe fear is the number one emotion that will keep us from God's plan and will for our lives. I don't think you need a doctorate degree to make that statement. You just need to think about your own life, and ask yourself what fear has kept you from doing.

Here I am again being very transparent (my next book will be my memoir), whew, wait for it!

Shortly after I was saved, I remember boasting, "I don't really deal with fear." Boy, did I get shown differently. When I was called by God to lead women's Bible studies and speak at my first ladies conference at church, it hit me. Oh, I will just set up, do the center-pieces for the tables, do all the behind-the-scenes stuff. Remember the story? Out of nowhere it came—the fear of speaking in public. I just could not do it! I wrestled with the Lord for about a year on this calling. *God, why had you called me to do this? Remember all the other talents you've given me—leadership, decorating, organizing, baking, managing—let me just do those things. But God...* This is where you realize and surrender yourself to let God do it through you.

You see, fear is the natural consequence of sin. Turn to Genesis 3:10.

He replied, "I heard you walking in the garden, so I hid. I was afraid because I was naked."

Here you have Adam in the garden after he and Eve committed the first sin, and they were hiding among the trees, afraid of what God was going to do to them.

Fear will keep us from doing a lot of things, like going up to someone sharing the gospel, even though we know, according to the Bible, that we are all commissioned to do so.

So, we know we have fear, the result of sin. Now let's look at 2 Timothy 1:7.

In this verse you see God doesn't give us that spirit of fear but of power, love, and self-discipline.

This gives us the boldness to come to the throne room without fear. This power comes from the confidence in the gospel. Here we must go back to Galatians 5:22-23 to see the fruits of the Spirit that are given to us and are within us all. And there is no room for fear here.

Scripture tells us over and over we must not fear. For many of us, we may have had our lives filled with fear, loss, unknowns (another fear I have, the unknown, but had to come to realize that). Maybe you are experiencing some of those fears as you are reading this. But now, amid this, one thing remains the same: the mission of God in our life and of those around us. Sometimes it is God's will for us to suffer, BUT GOD, we must have no fear. If we suffer for what is good, God is glorified.

Turn to 1 John 4:18. This verse states: "There is no fear in love, but perfect love casts out fear, because fear has to do with punishment, and whoever fears has not been perfected in love."

The NLT version of the Bible says it this way: "Such love has no fear, because perfect love expels all fear. If we are afraid, it is for fear of punishment [Genesis 3:10], and this shows that we have not fully experienced his perfect love."

Let that sink in for a minute. Go and worship to the song "Still Waters (Psalm 23)" by Leanna Crawford.

Welcome back. Let's continue.

The word "fear" appears at least 350 times in the Bible, depending on what version you are reading and what context of Scripture you are reading.

So, you ask, why do we have verses in the Bible that tell us to "fear the Lord"? Verses like Proverbs 9:10 that says, "The fear of the Lord is the beginning of wisdom."

Why would fearing the Lord give you wisdom? I thought fear was a negative emotion? Maybe these are questions you have asked yourself. I know I did until I really started studying the Bible and understanding what the word "fear" means in this particular verse.

The English word "fear" here is translated from the Hebrew word "yirah," which has a range of meanings in the Bible and means "awe" or "reverence" in this context. Fearing the Lord is a healthy fear that is rooted in respect for God's power and goodness. You see, before coming to follow Jesus, I had a fear of God as being this big overpowering man in the sky, waiting for me to mess up so He could send me straight to hell for my sins. Wow, did I have a lot of learning to do! Far from the truth, God draws us to Him through His love for us, not through "fearing" Him!

The fear of the Lord is the beginning of wisdom because feeling "awe" expands our perspective on any situation. As "awe" lifts our perspective beyond ourselves to God, we become wise by directing our attention to God rather than just ourselves or our situation. We can move past our "problems" and toward possibilities as we allow ourselves to grow in His wisdom and move toward possibilities like Matthew 19:26. What does this verse say? Yes, that "with God, all things are possible." Fearing God by having a sense of "awe" and "reverence" for His wonder helps us to be wise enough to stop placing limits on what all-powerful God can do in our lives. It helps us trust Him in deeper ways.

In closing this section, and I know it's been long and may have taken you longer to do than five days, I can't just leave this section on fear without pointing out other verses and helping to put "fear" (the negative emotion that grips us all and keeps us from doing God's will sometimes) back in its place!

Let's take another perspective of "fear." Have you ever thought of fear as an "idol"? It sure does get a front-row seat in our head and heart sometimes! Has fear ever called for your attention, resources, or talent? Has fear ever led you to make a decision? Or kept you from making one? Of course it has. Me too! Fear leads us to what feels safe and easy, maybe even a quick fix sometimes. And guess what? Sometimes fear, and the wisdom given of the fear, could keep you from making a big mistake. Think about a time when "fear" saved you from trouble. Write it below.

_____

_____

_____

Fear can keep us "stuck" and missing out on the wonderful things God has planned for our lives.

Remember over in section one of this study when we learned about the "deadly Ds"? One of those Ds goes hand in hand with fear, and that is distraction. Yes, distraction often works hand in hand with fear by putting words up in front of us like "can't" and "but" in order to keep us from walking with God to His fruitful places of blessing. I can't tell you how many times, before becoming a Christian and getting God's Word in me, that I boasted, "I don't deal with fear." God has shown me over and over since then that I do, in fact, deal with fear, just as we all do!

Back over in section one of the study, we also learned and studied the "I Am" statements. In this section we learned that God is the "Bread of Life" (John 6:35), the "Resurrection and the Life" (John 11:25), the "Good Shepherd" (John 10:11, 14), the "True Vine" (John 15:1), the "Gate for the Sheep" (John 10:7), and last, but certainly not least, the "door."

If you haven't heard the song "He Is," go look it up and let this song speak to your heart. When we know who "He Is" our fears and identities of who we are in Him are shored up! *Tetelestai*, which is Greek for the phrase, "It is finished" (John 19:30). No doubts, no fears, nothing should hold us back from walking in the power given to us through the blood of Jesus Christ! He did it for ALL of us on an old rugged cross, over two thousand years ago. He wants us to walk and live life in the fullness of Christ. Living without barriers, living in freedom from obstacles that keep us from God's best.

You see, we all deal with fear, worry, and anxiety; some of us more than others. I believe we have conditioned or sometimes made fear a "habit," the normal way of thinking. Like making this statement, "That's just who I am, I fear…" Again we have made fear an identity rather than something we can break through and take victory over.

Fear is not something new that just appeared one day out of nowhere. As you have seen, it's a consequence of sin. But God… The hope we have is that God's Word gives us EVERYTHING we need to fight against the fears that seem to come at us in the most inconvenient times. We do not have to live riddled with anxious thoughts, heart-pumping doubts, and mind-racing possibilities. We CAN live at peace with ourselves and with God, but we have to practice using a muscle. (Doesn't working out physically daily cause your muscles to get bigger?) Use your faith muscle daily. It doesn't mean we try to do more "good" than "bad," or check the box of our "holiness checklist" in hopes that we outdo someone less holy than us.

It simply means we turn to God's Word over and over again and receive the truth and the promises He gives us when fear threatens to take us down. It simply means we must TRUST and BELIEVE the Word of God.

That last bold statement is simple to put into words on paper. Is it that simple in your own life?

I guess by now you have the thought, *She sure is camping out here in fear,* and yes, I am. I have seen way too many times, in others, as well as my own life, missed opportunities when we don't use faith over fear.

Above you wrote about a time fear may have "saved" you from something dangerous. Now write or think about a time when fear kept you from doing something. Go on, write it. I know it's happened.

_____

_____

_____

You see, there will always be "barriers" to be broken down. We will experience many breakthroughs in our lives as we "overcome" (identity) the enemy and fulfill the will of God.

Let's look at 2 Corinthians 3:18: "So all of us who have had that veil removed can see and reflect the glory of the Lord. And the Lord—who is the Spirit—makes us more and more like Him as we are changed into His glorious image." Boom, there it is again—His image. This is what transformation looks like. The Holy Spirit's way of transformation works better and lasts longer than us trying to "change" our own selves.

Step by step, He works progressively on all of us on how to "do better," "think better," and live a life of freedom. This takes time for each of us. God works in His own timing. Don't compare your spiritual progress to anyone else's journey. You have your own roads to travel. Don't use anyone else's GPS; you have your own route! We will experience breakthroughs in our lives as we overcome the enemy and fulfill the will of God for our lives.

Let's look at Romans 1:17. Here again, an action-packed verse, and it comes after a "refrigerator verse." Remember what a refrigerator verse is? We learned that back in week 5.

Romans 1:17 says this: "This Good News tells us how God makes us right in his sight. This is accomplished from start to finish by faith. [BOOM!] As the Scriptures say, 'It is through faith that a righteous person has life.'"

What does that verse say, and what does it mean to you?

_____

_____

_____

Now look at Psalm 18:28-29: "You light a lamp for me. The Lord, my God, lights up my darkness. In your strength I can crush an army; with my God I can scale any wall."

Do you believe this verse today?

Journal what "wall" you need to jump over today. What thought do you need to take captive and break free from? Ask yourself what "fear" in your mind has control over you?

_____

_____

_____

F-E-A-R

has two meanings:

"Forget Everything And Run"

or

"Face Everything And Rise"

Which "Choice" Will You Make?

The End

I believe God is calling us to be "pioneers." King and Country has a song out titled "Pioneers," and so does Beckah Shae. Beckah's song "Pioneer" is my personal favorite! Two different artists, but nonetheless, both songs are calling us to "take the lead."

Upon the word "pioneer" being spoken to me, I started doing some research, writing a book. Careful, you will find yourself chasing rabbits down a hole, and you will be buried! And nine months later you will have hundreds of articles, a mess on your kitchen table, a summer that went by without you, and two close deaths, so you have those emotions to deal with. Also, I want to add here, writing a book can almost make you feel lonely. I know that may not make sense, but the enemy uses his tactics to keep you in your own thoughts. Thoughts like, no one understands me. Loneliness can be felt at different times in our lives. This was my year for that. But God…

I found a video on Facebook called "Pioneers" from a pastor from Word of Life Church, dated January 26, 2022. It really got me thinking. And once again, I find myself going down a rabbit hole. Let me get back on track! Pioneers! Pioneers! Pioneers!

Let's define the word "pioneer."

Oxford dictionary defines it like this: (noun) a person who is among the first to explore or settle a new country or area; (verb) to develop or be the first to use or apply (a new method, area of knowledge, or activity).

Boom, there you have it. God is calling us to action using this word as a verb. He is calling us to take the lead. We are CREATED in His Image by a CREATOR. Think about that. Jesus was a pioneer Himself. He was the very first pioneer. Look at Hebrews 12:1-3. Jesus is described as: "The source of salvation, the pioneer of living by faith, and the perfecter of living by faith." What is God calling you to "create"? No, we will not be creators of the earth, or the stars, or humans, or animals, or anything else that was created by our awesome God. But you are MADE in His image, and you have a creative mind. It's time for you to use it. Taylor Swift created a billion-dollar industry with song lyrics containing mostly heart-break. What can you "create" using the mind of a Sovereign God who designed you for His purposes? What new "land" will you let Him lead you to "pioneer"?

So, you ask, how do I become a pioneer? Well, first we must trust God's plan. Proverbs 3:5-6 says, "Trust in the Lord, with ALL your heart." We learned back in week 6 that "leaning on our own understanding" is where our "feelings" are.

Becoming pioneers is going to take some "work." It means plunging into an "unknown" territory, just as the early pioneers did. They had no idea what the land was like when they came across mountains, lakes, rivers, harsh weather, disease outbreaks, and so much more. When they got to a place, they began clearing the land, setting up camp, building communities and churches, leaving a legacy. Now, I don't intend for this to become a history lesson

Will you be a Settler?
A Museum Keeper?
Or a Pioneer?
God isn't asking you to
figure it all out.
He's asking you to

TRUST

that He already has!

on pioneers; I am simply saying that if we want to point people to Jesus, we CANNOT FEAR the unknown.

If God told us everything, we would not have to "walk by faith." Every single person used by God in the Bible was a pioneer, moved to an "area" they knew nothing about, into the "unknown."

Some people will never obey God's leading because of what? Fear of the unknown! Yes, the unknown stops us in our tracks, causing us to miss the blessing God has for us.

Faith is obeying God even when there is the element of the unknown. Faith obeys, even when you don't "feel" like it.

We learned in Hebrews 11 the great examples of faith. Let's look at Hebrews 11:1-3 now. Read it. What does it say? Faith shows the reality of what we hope for. Ever thought that God put that dream in your heart for your good and His glory? Verse two says that "through their faith, the people in the days of old [pioneers who went into the unknown] earned a good reputation. By faith, we understand the entire universe was formed at God's command, that what we now see did not come from anything that can be seen."

You simply cannot please God without faith. The need for "security" and "comfort" LIMITS the ability of God to move in your life.

Are you willing to take risks and confront the devil? Are you willing to press on to the possibilities ahead? Are you ready to have that pioneer spirit and "move" to where God is calling you? Some people are afraid to move, thinking, *Oh no, I can't move overseas.* God is not calling everyone overseas; He may be calling you to create the next greatest invention. What if Elon Musk had said, "I can't." Look at the empire he has built.

Pioneers are continually pressing on into new territory. Let God lead you one step at a time. Trust in Him; do not lean into your own understanding. Your own understanding will keep you right where you are, in your comfort zone, what feels "good." Step out in faith and become the "pioneer" God made you to be. Have that pioneering spirit. Move. Press on!

There are three "types" of people in the faith: pioneers, settlers, and museum keepers.

We have defined pioneers. Let's define settlers. The early settlers were defined as: a person who moves to a new place with the intention to stay there.

Are you a "settler" in your faith? Someone who made a new move and stopped? Did you stop too soon because you don't care what's over the next mountain or beyond the valley? Have you become "fearful" of what others will think of you when you mention God? Because the enemy has you believing that your current circumstances are all God has for you? That you are "stuck" in your own little world and can't move, so you are just going to "pitch a tent" and camp out? Not press on beyond the mountain that you can't "jump" high enough to see over?

Do you have the "settler" mindset of faith?

Or maybe you are a museum keeper? What is the job of a museum keeper. They "dust" off the memories of previous generations and talk about the exploits of the past. Are you stuck in the past? Dusting the memories of those gone before you? Content with not being a pioneer? It's time to let the past go—you don't live there anymore—and move on to the great unknown. That is where you will find Jesus. You will not find Him in the past, nor "settling" for your comfort zone. The end of YOU and your "feelings" is the beginning of where you will find Jesus.

You must be willing to face the giants as they come, and they will! We live in a world where we have "lost" our way as God's people, and the Lord is calling us back on track, back on the trail. What will it take for you to believe in the Lord and ignite the mindset of a pioneer? What will it take for YOU to impact this generation and leave the legacy of a pioneer? That is going to look different for ALL of us, BUT NONE of us will do it without keeping on moving, pressing on. Not becoming settlers or museum keepers, living in the past. The settlers were much needed to stay behind and let the early pioneers go ahead and explore more territory, which does not work when it comes to faith. We are ALL called to be pioneers.

So, you ask, how do I become a pioneer? How do I get this mindset of a pioneer? I am so glad you asked! Let me show you how I believe it can happen!

The key to becoming a pioneer is first allowing God to light the candle in your spirit. When your spirit is not lit by God, you cannot break through every barrier. The spirit of faith is a fire. God is a consuming fire. Hebrews 12:29 says, "For our God is a consuming fire."

There is a big difference between the flame of a candle and the roaring blast of a forest fire. Will you be the flame of a candle or the blast of a forest fire? Be consumed with the fire of God; allow Him to light the fire within you. How many fires do you think the pioneers had to light?

I referred to a song earlier in the study by Unspoken: "Start a Fire." In verse 1, it says, "This world can be cold and bitter, feels like we're in the dead of winter, waiting on something better. But am I really gonna hide forever? Over and over again, I hear your voice in my head. Let your light shine. Let your light shine for all to see."

Will you let God light your spirit? Proverbs 20:27 says, "The Lord's light penetrates the human spirit, exposing every hidden motive." Allow God to light your candle today. The spirit of faith is a fire in the spirit of us! We have to allow the Word of God to burn in our hearts, to enable us to OVERCOME in every area of our life. Once you let the Spirit light your flame, there are characteristics of a pioneer spirit that all of us have to possess in order to advance God's Kingdom. We ALL have places and space to "move to." We all have lands to settle. Don't get stuck; move on to your dreams.

Being a pioneer takes courage. We must be "agents of change," take the lead, and prepare the way for others to follow. Romans 12:1-2 tells us to not conform to our culture but to change it by being salt and light (Matthew 5:13-14).

We must be willing to be different, to "stand out," not fit in! You can't just go with the flow. You must decide to be different. Not a conformist but a "reformer." Reject peer pressure. You must choose to have the spirit of Caleb in the Old Testament. Numbers 14:24 says, "But my servant Caleb has a different attitude than the others have. He has remained loyal to me, so I will bring him into the land he explored." This promise was fulfilled in Joshua 14:6-15 when Caleb received his inheritance and was rewarded for his obedience. Caleb trusted God for his victory. What victory are you trusting God for today? Are you wholeheartedly committed to obey God?

We must be committed to doing the right thing. Doing the right thing isn't usually complicated, but it may cost you something.

2 Timothy 2:4 says, "Soldiers [pioneers], don't get tied up in the affairs of civilian life [settlers], for then they cannot please the officer who enlisted them." Verse 5 says, "And athletes cannot win the prize unless they follow the rules." Are you willing to follow the rules and obey His commands? It's definitely a choice we all have to make!

We must realize NO PRICE is too great to pay. Think about the disciples, some of the first pioneers. They left all that was comfortable when Jesus asked them to follow Him. Most of them martyred for their faith as they persisted to preach the gospel far and wide. We may not be called to make that kind of sacrifice here in America, while that is still happening overseas. Look at the believers of Afghanistan at this very moment. We must be willing to lose everything for Christ, if need be! William Wilberforce worked for four decades to abolish the slave trade in the British Empire. His work cost him a lot: his health, many sleepless nights, the ridicule of his peers, and the consternation of the people that were profiting from the slave trade. It was just three days before his death that he saw his work pay off and the vote cast to end slavery passed. Was he born for "such a time as this"?

Pioneers have the heart of a warrior. We must have the Spirit of David and his men in the Bible. We may not have to fight physically, but we may have to battle against the powers of darkness. We learned earlier in the study, in Ephesians, how we have to "suit up" and put on the full armor of God. Pioneers cannot sit on the sidelines and do nothing. We must stand up and take action for God and His Word, whatever it requires! Doing this, we must realize that wisdom given by God is mightier than strength. Turn to Proverbs 24:5-6: "The wise are mightier than the strong, and those with knowledge grow stronger and stronger. So don't go into war without wise guidance; victory depends on having many advisers." An athlete who thinks clearly, who assesses his plans and strategies, has an advantage over a physically strong person. That's why God chooses to put people with wisdom in some situations and not necessarily muscle. Think about that. It's great to have muscle, but the prior verse tells us that wisdom is better to have. Where and how do you gain wisdom? Since wisdom is a vital part of strength, it pays to attain it! Do you think David had wisdom? Yes, the Bible depicts him as a wise leader who made wise decisions. What did David do before going into battle? Yes, he asked God for directions. Don't go before first asking God for direction. His GPS is the way!

WE MUST BE WILLING to go into the UNKNOWN. Jesus said, GO (Matthew 28:19). I can't find anywhere in the Bible where it says to "be comfortable." Many of us have become settlers, settled into our routines, what makes us feel good or looks good to others. Settlers are not willing to take risks and venture into uncharted territory. When God's mission statement is no longer our mission statement, then something is wrong. We are comfortable where we are! This is why I believe many churches have not grown or failed. They have "settled" because of fear of the unknown and not moved! Luke chapter 14 tells us the cost of following Jesus. Read it someday soon.

Pioneers have extreme passion. People may tell you things like, you need to be less intense. I received the word "radical" shortly after I was saved. And I am certain someone has looked at me and said, "Why does she raise her hands and move around so much during worship?" Do it anyway! Dive into the biblical account of the heart of King David in 2 Samuel 6, where David is recorded as dancing and jumping around with ALL his might before the Lord in a simple linen ephod, not dressed as a king, unable to keep his joy inside. When was the last time you showed passion for Jesus? What does passion look like to you? When have you allowed the love of God to compel you to have no choice but to lift a hand in praise? Be a David, run to the GIANTS while everyone is running away, for fear of being made a "FOOL" of yourself!

Pioneers are willing to fight for a cause bigger than themselves. If your personal needs or wants in life are more important than the cause God has called you to accomplish, you will NEVER be a pioneer! Read that again. Do you always have to have the feeling of safety? Comfort? We must be fully devoted to Christ and advancing His Kingdom. We must not be satisfied with the status quo. We must long to make a difference, be a world changer, be a light in the dark. Invest our entire lives to doing it.

Beckah Shae has a song called "Legacy," and the lyrics say this: "How can you say that the world is in a terrible state when you haven't done anything? The role that you play could be a hero or a villain. It's on you, and every day could be your last scene. What good is love if you don't give it to somebody else? All that you learned is no good to you if you keep it to yourself. And what's victory if you can't stand with someone else? A legacy. Hangs on to you and me to teach each other well. Who will it be? Who will plant the seeds and lead to see others lead, paving the way to dream bigger dreams? What sacrifice, to lay down your life and leave courage for someone else to rise. But it's so worth it, to keep this legacy." (Will you leave courage laying around for someone else to pick up? This line alone challenged me to RISE!)

It continues back to the chorus and then says this: "So here's a thank you to the heroes, the leaders, and the brave ones who made a way for us to know the truth. You are the champions, and we're the generation that will forever honor you! Legacy!"

Will you lead the way? Be a pioneer?

I leave you with this. Go listen to the song "Pioneer" by Beckah Shae. You can't listen to it and not MOVE! GO! The freedom is there waiting for you. Be a risk taker, a creator. Make new discoveries. Dream big. You will only make new discoveries. Find out what's on the other side of the mountain. Take the risk and see what God has for you. God's blessing is only received through obedience!

Instead of worrying about what people say of you, why not spend time trying to accomplish something they will admire?

— Dale Carnegie

What legacy do you want to leave?

In Closing

What is the key to moving past fear, comparing ourselves to others, not being jealous of others and their gifts and talents? What is the secret to moving into our own identity and walking away from fear?

Turn to 1 John 5:21. Apostle John closes this book with this sentence: "Dear Children [our identity in Christ], keep away from anything that might take God's place in your hearts."

This is a loaded sentence; many things can take God's place in our lives. Could fear be one of those things? This could be ANYTHING that denies Christ's fullness in you. Anything that substitutes for true faith. Any human idea that claims your thoughts and claims authority over the Bible and the truth of Scripture. Any loyalty that replaces God at the center of our lives.

Ask yourself the question about your own life this very day! It could be an addiction, fear, sin, jealousy, comparison, people pleasing, etc. This is going to look different for all of us.

What may be keeping you from being that pioneer, that leader, from believing you were made with purpose, for purpose?

1 John paints a clear picture of who Jesus Christ is. What we think about Jesus is central to our teaching, preaching, and living.

My hope through this study is that you have first learned "who He is" and "who you are" in Him.

I hope that you have learned that Jesus is the God man, fully human and fully God at the same time. He came to earth to die in our place for sins. That through faith in Him, we are given eternal life and the POWER to do His will.

What is your answer to the most important question you could ever ask yourself: "Who is Jesus Christ?"

First, ask yourself that question, and then ask yourself, "Am I walking in the newness of life (Romans 6:4), promised to me at new birth (2 Corinthians 5:17)? What 'thing' is it that I am allowing to keep me from the JOY that John longs for us to experience?" (Or better yet, your Saviour!)

In this sentence, it's as if God lifts our chin and looks into our eyes here to say, *Don't let ANYTHING lead you astray from the best I have for you!*

Yes, given to us by the Lord. How can we break through the chains of defeat, doubt, and insecurity?

We live in a society that seems to be afraid and uncomfortable with people and things we are unable to categorize. Therefore, we have created "labels" based on our mental capacity, physical appearance, religious beliefs, political beliefs, ethnicity, and more.

We have to come to realize that EVERYONE is uniquely made by God, so it is okay to be complex in who we are and not grouped by where society places us.

We are in the social media era that tells us twenty likes is not enough. When was the last time you received twenty compliments in one day? Imagine getting twenty compliments a day in "real life." Your head would be so big, you couldn't carry it, right? Jesus is enough. You don't need all those "likes." He came to you in your time of "need." Met you right where you are, "in a mess," picked you up and placed you on the road to a place called Heaven.

I'm good. I don't need to go to any social media outlet and make myself "known."

Labels constrict us and force us to "fit" into a certain stigma. The smart one, the introvert, the extrovert, the Hispanic, the White, the Black, the athlete, Gen X, Gen Z, senior adult, child, the Christian (boy, this one can be hard to live up to), toddler… I could go on and on with these labels.

All of these labels show one side of who a person really is. For example, if you go to the web and search "Gen Z," boy, oh boy, this generation is doomed by the world view. Anxiety ridden, no hope, lazy, depressed because they had to face a pandemic (we all did), fearful, anxious, insecure, and the labels will just continue on and on. I choose not to read these articles; they are the world's view of people.

Did you know that, according to a Pew Research Center report dated January 26, 2018, no official commission or group decides what generation is called what and when it starts and when it ends. These "labels" are designed mainly for marketing purposes. (This is not in the article; this is my take on them after running a business for many years.) These labels are used for reaching a certain age group to "reach" them through marketing goods and services. For example, why would a pharmaceutical company advertise arthritis medication to Gen Z and not Baby Boomers? Gen Z is not ready for that yet! Only two big companies call their consumers users: social media companies and drug dealers. Watch what label you let someone define you. Maybe you are facing one of these labels today. And guess what? You might not be Gen Z. You may be a Millennial, a Baby Boomer, Gen Y, or any other label.

I bet you could talk to the guy and girl from high school who received the "best dressed" award, and they may tell you that the expectation and pressure to always look good came with great pressures to live up to that label.

This is why we cannot be defined by one label or a hundred likes.

If we are constantly viewing the "best dressed" and that and only that, we may not see our other qualities, or we may not be known for our faith. While there is nothing wrong with having this label, we cannot let this label, or any other, define who we are.

We must change our viewpoint on labels. The Bible tells us in our key verse for this study, Psalms 139:13, that we are created in our mother's womb. Before we took our first breath, God had molded us and determined where every single freckle on our skin and hair on our head would go. Verse 14 says, "I praise you, for I am fearfully and wonderfully made. Wonderful are your works; my soul knows it very well." Despite how the world sees us, God sees us for who we really are. We must accept this true statement and not fall into the enemy's trap.

I believe it is important to be aware and learn about the labels placed upon us as we go through life and society. But labels have a way of removing us from seeing who a person really is and maybe as seeing yourself for who you really are. We are always changing in life, going through different cycles, and because of this we might not "fit" a certain label anymore. Just as we grow from child to adult. Obviously, things change, but wouldn't it be easier to merely understand that we are made by an almighty CREATOR, and because of this we do not need to worry about how others might label us?

Ultimately, as having the label of "Christian," have you ever asked yourself the question, "Was I made to stand out? Should I stand out?"

We all know that one person who dresses a certain way, whether it's wearing a whacky-looking tie or dress. Maybe it's so bright it looks like it runs on batteries. You know them. Think about that one person right now in your mind. Why do you think they do this? What is their purpose?

Well, I don't want you to focus on that person today. I want to point you to Scripture today that tells you you were made to stand out!

Jesus wants to see us stand out from the crowd. He does not want us to get stuck on just being a Gen Z or Gen X, an anxiety-ridden, hopeless generation. He wants us to change the world. Move on from what we left at the altar. Move on from the label of young or old. I have come to the conclusion that Jesus wants to see us stand out from the crowd, speak the truth in love (Ephesians 4:15). This verse means speaking the truth in a way that is doctrinally correct, biblically committed, and done in love for the benefit of others. If you do this you are going to "stand out." We are meant to stand out! So you ask yourself, "Why stand out?" Now, I'm not saying we should dress differently for the attention or spotlight. We have another purpose for standing out in this world. Matthew 5:16 says, "In the same way, let your light shine before men, so they see your good works and give glory to your Father in Heaven." Lights shine bright, especially in the dark!

1 Peter 3:15 says, "Always be prepared to give an answer to everyone who asks you to give the reason for the hope you have."

If we believe these two verses alone, then we know that we are going to glow in a dark world. Where society and sin have normalized and try to indoctrinate us to believe that is just "who the world is right now," and we must conform to it. Romans 12:2 tells us to not conform to the world but to be transformed by the renewing of your mind. This is a DAILY action; faith is an action.

No, we are not called to "fit into the world." God has called us to be different. To stand against the grain. To be the city on a hilltop (Matthew 5:14-16).

In today's self-seeking world, being "liked" and "wanted" is something we ALL yearn for, no matter if we are a Baby Boomer or Gen Z. We all yearn for this. And admit it or not, it's how culture forces us to "feel" and our culture advertises us to "feel." It's all about how we "feel" nowadays. How do you think Jesus felt standing out in a crowd? He did, you know!

Our purpose for being here on earth, for even existing, is to point others toward God. We are here to bring Him glory. This can happen through our behaviors, our actions, and our decisions. We will not bring Him glory if we blend in and look like the world around us. We must stand out, causing others to see us and wonder why we stand out. Not because of the clothes we wear, the color we wear our hair, the beliefs we have, although others need to know what we "stand" for.

As I am typing this today, a text just came to my phone, and this is what it read: "If you don't speak out against the abortion pill coming to your local pharmacy, you may never get the chance again. Act now: link to go there and speak out."

Folks, I believe that God put us here for, "such a time as this" (Esther 4:14). To speak the truth in love on topics such as abortion, homosexuality, the transgender movement, and all the other "women's rights" movements. Jeremy Camp has a wonderful song titled, "These Days." It is a great song telling us that maybe we were made for these days. That God calls us by name and challenges us to think and ask the question, "What?"

You may be asking these or more questions. God may be calling you to trust Him and step out in faith!

Why am I at a job I hate? Why am I not the popular girl at school? Why did my mom die when I was ten, leaving an alcoholic father to raise me? Why was I born into such a dysfunctional family? Why? Why? Why? Think about your situation; the questions could go on and on. We ALL have them!

I believe that we will not do this, out of fear of what others may think of us, if we are NOT allowing God to SHINE through us and stand out. There will be times that the choice between "blending in" and "standing out" can be scary. The temptation to "play it safe" and blend in will always be there. This behavior is short-term thinking. We must break FREE from this kind of thinking and "stand out." He is calling us to stand out. He is real and wants us to be fully committed to Him. 2 Chronicles 16:9 says, "The eyes of the Lord search the whole earth in order to strengthen those whose hearts are fully committed to him. What a fool you have been! From now on you will be at war."

He wants us fully committed to Him, for His purposes. If we do it, He will get the glory, and we will one day be rewarded. If we shy away and blend in, we will miss the opportunity to see Him act. If we do this, where is our faith? Do we really believe what we say we believe? Do we really BELIEVE, and are we confident that He who started a good work in us will see it to completion (Philippians 1:6)?

Do you believe Deuteronomy 31:6? "So be strong and courageous! Do not be afraid and do not panic before them. For the Lord you God will personally go with you; He will neither fail you nor abandon you."

Or Deuteronomy 31:8? "The Lord himself goes before you and will be with you; He will never leave you nor forsake you. Do not be afraid; do not be discouraged."

Do you believe that He has already gone before you? Are you ready to step out of your comfort and into the unknown?

He will make you SHINE for your cause.

Psalm 37:6: "He will make your innocence radiate like the dawn, and the justice of your cause will shine like the noonday sun." Boy, think about that. How bright is the noonday sun?

I am actually sitting here now enjoying the noonday sun on this beautiful fall afternoon, thinking I am going to have to move from the sun because it is too hot.

When have you been so bright that you caused someone to move from the heat or the darkness? Loaded question, but one we all should ask ourselves! What is the explanation of this verse? I'm glad you asked. This verse means that if a person TRUSTS in God, DELIGHTS in God, and GIVES their burdens to God, God will vindicate them. God will show the believers righteousness as clearly as light reveals everything it shines on. Could this mean if we do "our job" He will do His? Could this be a call to ACTION? Faith is a verb here.

We must stop looking around us and start looking up, allowing God to teach us how to do that. You were made for important work. No person, label, or thing can ever change this truth. Start walking in that truth today! You are His treasure designed for His good works and purposes.

God's labels are so much MORE than man's labels. Let Him define you today with such labels as chosen, beautiful, redeemed, His children, loved, forgiven, created in His Image, liberated, members of God's family, forever known, His handiwork, righteous, and so much more.

Fill in your favorite label (or name because, after all, you are truly "named by God.")

_____

_____

_____

My greatest love and blessings are prayed for you today! November 14, 2024. 3:15 p.m. Nine months and ten days after the Lord put into my spirit a book called *What Was I Made For?* inspired by a Billie Eilish song, made for the *Barbie* movie. Who would have thought that God would use me and that song to put so much into this! When that was spoken to me, I knew it was for a book. But I had been thinking of writing a memoir for years, just never thought I had the "sense" enough to write a book. And, you know what? I didn't. But He did! My very independent little self tried really hard, even here, to do it on my own strength. It didn't work! I became very angry and felt defeated many, many times this year. Not like I haven't been there before, but just as before. BUT GOD... My two favorite words in the Bible.

I pray that through this study you learned first who Jesus is and then who you are in Him.

I have included some "young pioneers," and some who have gone before us, and when you read their stories, you will have to know that these people or the people of the Bible are no different than you or me. They just lifted their chins up, did hard things, and didn't quit when the going got tough! They looked to the author of their salvation and "pioneered." They moved when it wasn't comfortable and stepped out into the unknown. I challenge you to do the same!

Look me up on Instagram and Facebook.

I would love to see pictures of you standing in the mirror, telling the devil where to "shove it" and "who you are" in Christ! Flood social media with these pics and positive statements about yourself. Not because you need or want the "likes" but because you know who He is and who you are in Him. One spark could start a fire. Do it, light the match! Start the fire! Remember the biggest trick of the enemy is putting "fear" in you. Stand in front of a mirror now, go listen to "The Breakup Song" by Francesa Battistelli. Boldly claim that you are not owned by fear and will not be held by it! Break up with that "boyfriend" today!

Go and listen to "Oceans" by Hillsong United. Listen to the words of this song and pray it over yourself. Word of caution, once you give Him permission, buckle up. He will take you "Into the Wild" (Josh Baldwin), another song calling you to faith and trust! Follow Him today! Let's go!

The World
Needs
Who You
Are Called
to Be.

For the Young Reader

The world is telling our young people that they are anxiety ridden, that their mental health will not allow them to do big things for God. The Bible tells us differently. In instances all throughout the Bible you will see young people doing big things.

1 Timothy 4:12: "Let no one despise your youth, but be an example to those who believe, in speech, in conduct, in love, in faith, in purity."

I challenge the young reader to look up the stories of the following young people, starting with the Bible examples and then the more modern individuals.

Pioneers from the Bible

Daniel

In his teens, the Babylonians took him captive and placed him in a three-year Babylonian education. The Babylonian culture attempted to stamp out any previous Israelite identity he had. Sound a bit like our school system?

Still, he stood his ground and refused to eat the food presented to him, which would defile him (Daniel 1:8). Upon risk of death, he refused, but the Lord rewarded him for his faithfulness. He ends up affecting change, and the entire palace diet shifts because of him (Daniel 1:16).

Jeremiah

At a mere seventeen years of age, Jeremiah finds himself called into the position of a prophet who had a marred history in Israel. Jeremiah laments his inadequacy for public speaking because of his young age (Jeremiah 1:6), but God doesn't let him use this excuse. We may feel inadequate because of our age in any setting: work, church, a friend group. But God will go with you, just as He did Jeremiah.

Esther

In her teens, Esther saves her nation. Facing death herself to confront the king, she ends up reversing a law intended to wipe out her people. Esther proves that teenagers can change the world for God's Kingdom, even when the world seems to wipe out that same Kingdom.

Miriam

The young girl Miriam ensures her brother's safety on the Nile River as he lands in the hands of the pharaoh's daughter. Even though the pharaoh sought to slaughter all the Hebrew male infants, the daughter takes pity on him. Miriam volunteers her own mother to nurse her brother Moses (Exodus 2:9) and ends up not only saving his life but saving the life of her people in Exodus.

The Bible has lots more young people who did "big hard things" for Christ. Whether you are nine or twenty-nine or fifty-nine, these figures can exemplify how you can live a life for Christ at any age.

Find your favorite young Bible character. Read up on them, and challenge yourself to step out in faith. This may look different than you could ever imagine! "For my thoughts are not your thoughts, neither are your ways my ways, saith the LORD. For as the heavens are higher than the earth, so are my ways higher than your ways and my thoughts than your thoughts" (Isaiah 55:8-9).

Let that register in your thoughts, go in your mind—the thought of how far earth is from Heaven. We serve a BIG GOD! Thank Him today for His ways being higher than our own.

Modern Pioneers

Louis Braille

The Braille language for the blind was developed by Louis Braille in 1824 when he was just fifteen years old. He tweaked and expanded it after that, but having been blind himself since the age of three, he was inspired at a young age to conceive of a way to read and write. Braille consists of a code of sixty-three characters, each made of one to six raised dots arranged in a six-position matrix or cell. The dots are embossed on paper and are read by using one's fingers. He later adapted the Braille system to cover musical notation as well. He published the first Braille book, a three-volume history book, in 1837. Think he had to do "hard things"?

Malala Yousafzai

"I tell my story not because it's unique, but because it is the story of many girls." She was born in Pakistan in 1997. Welcoming a baby girl is not always cause for celebration in Pakistan. Her father was a teacher. When the Taliban took control of her town in the Swat Valley, they banned many things: owning a television, playing music, etc. And they enforced harsh punishment for those who defied their orders. And they said girls could no longer go to school. In January 2008, at just eleven years old, she said goodbye to her classmates, not knowing when, if ever, she would see them again.

In 2012, at age fifteen, Malala spoke out publicly on behalf of girls and their right to learn. This made her a target. In October 2012, on her way home from school, a masked gunman boarded her school bus and asked, "Who is Malala?" He then shot her on the left side of her head. She woke up ten days later in a hospital in Birmingham, England.

In 2014, after months of surgery and rehabilitation, she joined her family in their new home in the UK.

She had a choice at this time to live a quiet life or make the most of this new life she felt like she had been given. She was determined to continue her fight until every girl could go to school. With her father's help, she established the Malala Fund, a charity dedicated to giving every girl an opportunity to achieve a future she chooses. In recognition of their work, she became the youngest-ever Nobel laureate and received the Nobel Peace Prize in December 2014, at the age of seventeen.

In 2018, she began studying philosophy, politics, and economics at the University of Oxford. In 2020, she graduated from Oxford University. With more than 130 million girls out of school today, she continues to fight for education and equality. Her vision is to create a world where all girls can learn and lead.

Malala invites you to join her in her fight for girls' education on her website at Malala.org.

Sara Barratt

Sara Barratt is an author, speaker, and Jesus follower. Her passion is to encourage her peers to live wholeheartedly for Christ. She knows how hard it is to follow Jesus in our culture. She says that Jesus has completely, radically, 100 percent changed her life.

At age eighteen she wrote her first book, *Love Riot: A Teenage Call to Live With Relentless Abandon for Christ.* It's a battle cry from one teen to another to live with relentless abandon for Jesus, no matter the cost.

Since then, she has authored several books, including *Stand Up, Stand Strong*, a book challenging readers, no matter their age, to boldly stand up for the truth of the Bible. She believes that God calls us to boldly engage our upside-down culture through the lens of His truth.

Robby Novak

Robby is an American actor and media personality best known for portraying Kid President on YouTube and on television. Born October 24, 2003, in Henderson, Tennessee, he and his sister Lexi were adopted by David and Lori Novak.

In July 2012, on the channel SoulPancake, he released his first YouTube video, which, as of March 2023, had 48 million views. It is titled "A Pep Talk from Kid President to You."

Novak is featured in a series of YouTube videos and in a television show produced by actor Rainn Wilson. Novak's first YouTube clip as Kid President, written and directed by his brother-in-law Brad

Montague, was uploaded in the summer of 2012. In October 2019, Novak and Montague started a series titled "Are We There Yet?" which shows Novak and Montague's trip around the United States in which they meet children who are trying to "Make the World a Little More Awesome."

Novak suffers from osteogenesis imperfecta, a condition where his bones break easily. As a result, Novak has had over seventy broken bones and several major surgeries. Think he's done any "hard things"?

Alex and Brett Harris

These twin brothers founded TheRebelution.com when they were just sixteen years old. They had no idea it would soon become one of the most popular Christian teen websites on the Internet, with nearly 40 million page views from over 5 million visitors since 2007. At seventeen, the twins had the opportunity to intern under State Supreme Court Justice Tom Parker, becoming the youngest interns on record at the Alabama Supreme Court. This age-defining experience convinced them young people are far more capable than society suggests. At eighteen they co-authored their first book, *Do Hard Things: A Teenage Rebellion Against Low Expectations*. It has reached number one under Christianity and since has sold over four hundred thousand copies and has been translated into a dozen languages. Their ongoing aim is to follow Jesus Christ wherever He leads them. I encourage all young readers to read their book and "do hard things!"

Acknowledgements

hank you to my Lord and Savior for entrusting me to not only speak and teach His Word, but now write for Him. His Word is living and active (Hebrews 4:12), and I am thankful for being "fearfully and wonderfully" made! I was "Made For More."

Thank you to my husband Perry for his support through the writing and publishing process. Thanks for all your support that led up to the final day of publishing. I love you Perry.

Thank you, Mason Leonard (Youth Pastor Mt.Pisgah Baptist Church). Mason, you unknowingly help write this book through your teachings on Wednesday nights. Every single time through the year 2024, you took the stage to preach, the Lord used you as His vessel to speak His Word. May God bless you!

Thanks to Chad Campbell (Lead Pastor Mt. Pisgah Baptist Church).Chad also unknowingly helped to write this book through his Sunday morning sermons. Both he and Mason had no idea I was writing a book. This is how you can tell the Pastor is "in tuned" to the Lord, when he speaks to the congregation through his sermons. Thank you Chad!

Thank you to my daughter Tiffany. Tiffany made me Mother at the ripe old age of 18, and while our life was not always easy, the lessons that I learned along the way are a BIG part of why I believe the Lord chose me as His servant, to write for Him. Love you always Tiffany!

To my other children, Melissa and Richard. Although we are a blended family, the lessons you guys have shown me also contributed to me being who I am today, and I would not trade those lessons for anything! Thank you!

To my four grandchildren, Cole, Cooper, Sampson, and Camden. Thanks for giving me some of the greatest memories of my life! Love you guys BIG!

Thanks to Pastor Terry and Angel Rogers, Faith Renewed Church, Mauldin, SC. Terry allowed me to start a group called "Transformation" at his church. I led this group of ladies for four years. This group laid the foundation and helped me to grow into the birth of "Radically Sweet Transformation."(10 Years Later). Many thanks to them!

To George Stevens, book designer. George was very patient and understanding throughout this whole process. His professionalism and keen knowledge of publishing and design brought this book to life, and I appreciate all his help throughout the whole publishing process.

To Nate Best, Copy Editor. Thanks to Nate for doing a hearty cleanup for both grammar and structure, without changing one single thing to the message of the book. Thank you Nate!

Scan this QR code to access a Spotify playlist containing songs reerenced in this book!